KU-036-791

Home Office Research Study 203

An evaluation of the use and effectiveness of the Protection from Harassment Act 1997

Jessica Harris

Research, Development and Statistics Directorate
Home Office

Home Office Research Studies

The Home Office Research Studies are reports on research undertaken by or on behalf of the Home Office. They cover the range of subjects for which the Home Secretary has responsibility. Titles in the series are listed at the back of this report (copies are available from the address on the back cover). Other publications produced by the Research, Development and Statistics Directorate include Research Findings, the Research Bulletin, Statistical Bulletins and Statistical Papers.

The Research, Development and Statistics Directorate

RDS is part of the Home Office. The Home Office's purpose is to build a safe, just and tolerant society in which the rights and responsibilities of individuals, families and communities are properly balanced and the protection and security of the public are maintained.

RDS is also a part of the Government Statistical Service (GSS). One of the GSS aims is to inform Parliament and the citizen about the state of the nation and provide a window on the work and performance of government, allowing the impact of government policies and actions to be assessed.

Therefore -

Research Development and Statistics Directorate exists to improve policy making, decision taking and practice in support of the Home Office purpose and aims, to provide the public and Parliament with information necessary for informed debate and to publish information for future use.

"The views expressed in this report are those of the authors, not necessarily those of the Home Office (nor do they reflect Government policy)."

First published 2000
Application for reproduction should be made to the Communications and Development Unit, Room 201, Home Office, 50 Queen Anne's Gate, London SW1H 9AT.

© Crown copyright 2000   ISBN   1 84082 499 9
ISSN   0072 6435

B

Foreword

Before the implementation of the Protection from Harassment Act, laws relating to stalking were inadequate. Whilst it was possible to prosecute the 'stalker' whose behaviour breached existing laws, nothing could be done about seemingly innocuous harassment which could be similarly upsetting and distressing to victims. The Act came into force in June 1997, and was intended to deal with the overt problem of stalking. The research outlined in this report was carried out to evaluate the use and effectiveness of the Act three years on. The most striking finding is that cases of stalking are actually relatively rare and the Act is being used for a variety of behaviour, including domestic and inter-neighbour disputes. Such cases are sometimes seen as more appropriate for civil proceedings which has implications for the criminal investigation and prosecution of harassment cases.

David Moxon
Crime and Criminal Justice Unit
Research, Development and Statistics Directorate

Acknowledgements

I am very grateful to the Crown Prosecution Service and the Lord Chancellor's Department who were instrumental in getting the research off the ground. I am also grateful to the Chief Constables as well as the Chief Crown Prosecutors who agreed to take part in this study and, in particular, those in the four areas who helped me with the research.

Particular thanks go to the liaison officers in each of the police forces who were very helpful and co-operative, as well as to my contacts in the CPS. I am also obliged to Ian Smith, one of the police officers involved in the investigation of the Tracey Morgan case and who was instrumental in the establishment of the Protection from Harassment Act.

I am indebted to all those who agreed to be interviewed for the study, including magistrates, CPS lawyers and caseworkers, the police and particularly to victims of harassment who agreed to talk about their experiences.

Thanks for valuable assistance goes to the Suzy Lamplugh Trust who have a particular interest in this area, and most certainly to Tracey Morgan who provided extremely valuable information from the victim's point of view.

Finally, I would like to thank my colleagues within RDS – David Brown for his extremely helpful advice and comments throughout the study, Pat Dowdeswell for her help and support with statistics and Robert Street for his helpful drafting comments as well as having to share a room with me during the writing of the report!

Jessica Harris

Contents

Summary of the main findings

Background

The Protection from Harassment Act came into force on 16 June 1997.[1] One of the Act's aims was to tackle the problem of 'stalking', but it also covered a range of behaviour, which might be classed more broadly as harassment of one kind or other.

The Act introduced two new criminal offences – a section 2 summary offence[2] which deals with conduct that amounts to harassment of another and a section 4 either-way offence[3] that covers situations where the victim fears that violence will be used. For both offences there must be a course of conduct. The court has the power to make a restraining order against those convicted in order to prevent a repetition of the harassmentt.

When the Act was implemented, the government gave an undertaking to evaluate its success in dealing with cases of harassment. This research was commissioned to evaluate the use and effectiveness of the Act.

Methodology

The study examined 167 Protection from Harassment cases sent by the police to the CPS during 1998 for a decision on prosecution. Using CPS files as the main source of information, details were recorded about the characteristics of each case and its progress through the criminal justice system.

Interviews were also carried out with police officers, Crown Prosecutors, magistrates and victims of harassment.

---

1   The full text of the Act is reproduced at Appendix 1.
2   Punishable by up to six months in prison or a maximum fine of £5,000 or both.
3   Punishable by up to five years in prison or an unlimited fine or both.

The nature of harassment cases

The study found that the Protection from Harassment Act is being used to deal with a variety of behaviour other than stalking, including domestic and inter-neighbour disputes, and rarely for stalking itself.

- The suspect and victim were known to each other in almost all cases, either as partners, ex-partners or relatives (41% of cases), acquaintances (41%) or neighbours (16%). In only four per cent were the parties strangers.

- The most common reason for harassment was that the complainant had ended an intimate relationship with the suspect.

- Eighty per cent of suspects were male; among victims almost the same proportion were female.

- The study identified several different types of behaviour which constituted harassment. These included:

  - threats (either face-to-face or by telephone)

  - a range of distressing behaviour, such as following the victim, waiting outside their house or making silent telephone calls

  - damaging the victim's property

  - use of violence

  - miscellaneous other actions, such as sending unwelcome gifts or ordering unwanted taxis on the complainant's behalf.

Police action

- Victims usually chose the police as their first port of call when they were subjected to harassment. However, many were unaware of the Act and the remedies available and had endured unwanted behaviour for a significant time before they reported it.

- The police must establish that a course of conduct amounting to harassment has occurred before they can make an arrest. In some cases they might wait until there had been a number of incidents, but in a minority they arrested (incorrectly) when there had apparently only been one.

- In most cases the statement of the victim provided valuable evidence, but it is important that there is corroboration so that the case does not depend only on the victim's word against that of the complainant. Among the important sources of evidence collected by the police were:

  ○ evidence from other eye-witnesses

  ○ documentary evidence (e.g. logs of incidents of harassment)

  ○ material or forensic evidence

  ○ medical evidence (e.g. of the psychological effect on the victim or of injuries)

  ○ records of prior police warnings issued to the suspect.

- Evidence of previous incidents was not always consistently recorded by the police or readily accessible to other officers who might get called to deal with similar situations involving the same parties.

- The police rarely approached the CPS for advice before charging a suspect. Partly this was because they suspected that the CPS might advise against proceedings but it was also because advice was readily available from senior officers.

- Nationally, roughly three times as many defendants are proceeded against for the less serious section 2 offence as for the section 4 offence. Officers interviewed suggested that it was easier to prove the lower level offence, since they did not have to show that the victim feared that violence would be used. However, they were not always clear as to the difference between the two offences.

- Most suspects charged and bailed (nearly 90%) were given bail conditions – usually designed to prevent them approaching the victim. Only seven per cent were kept in custody for court.

- The officers dealing with cases generally kept victims well informed up to the time of charge, but the provision of information was not always so good after this point. The lack of information at these later stages was felt by some victims to be one aspect of a wider problem of lack of support in helping them through the court process.

The prosecution process and court proceedings

- Thirty-nine per cent of harassment cases were terminated by the CPS, compared with the national average for all offences of 14 per cent (including bindovers). In nearly half of terminated cases the defendant agreed to be bound over. Cases involving neighbour disputes were the most likely to be dropped (nearly half).

- The great majority of terminations were on the grounds of insufficient evidence, most commonly where the victim retracted their complaint.

- Relatively few cases were picked up in which proceedings were dropped because of mental disorder on the part of the suspect. In the few cases where there were grounds to believe that the suspect was mentally disordered, practitioners felt that it was preferable (unless the disorder was severe) to proceed with the case in order to gain access to a restraining order if the case resulted in a conviction.

- As with those given police bail, most defendants bailed by the court were given bail conditions designed to keep them away from the victim. Over 20 per cent were known to have breached their bail conditions. Ten per cent were held in custody after their first court appearance.

- Where cases proceeded to a hearing, 63 per cent of defendants pleaded guilty. Of the remainder, 18 per cent were convicted following a contested trial, while the case against 16 per cent was dismissed. The remaining three per cent were committed to the Crown Court and all were convicted.

- Overall, the conviction rate in cases resulting in a hearing was 84 per cent.

- The sentence most frequently awarded was a conditional discharge (in 43% of convictions). However, this and other sentences were often accompanied by a restraining order (in just over half of convictions).

- Restraining orders were usually specified to run for 12 or 18 months and, like bail conditions, made stipulations designed to stop the offender continuing their harassing behaviour.

- Few breaches of restraining orders were picked up by the research. This was partly due to the limited follow-up period, but it also seems that breaches do occur but are not effectively policed.

Practitioners' views

- Most practitioners interviewed felt that the Protection from Harassment Act is a welcome piece of legislation, enabling intervention in cases of harassment where little could be done before. Magistrates felt confident in dealing with harassment cases although such cases were not common.

- The most important feature of the legislation was considered to be the restraining order, which was believed to provide protection for the victim. However, for restraining orders to be effective it was felt to be important:

  o   to inform victims of the order and its conditions

  o   to investigate all the circumstances of the harassment before framing the order

  o   to police breaches effectively.

Interviewees identified failings in each of these areas.

- There was some confusion among practitioners about when it was appropriate to use the criminal provisions of the Act rather than the civil remedy. These views were coloured by the perception of some that the Act had originally been introduced to deal with serious cases of stalking rather than domestic or inter-neighbour disputes.

- Among the other issues raised in interviews were:

  o   uncertainties among the police about when section 2 and section 4 charges were most appropriate

○ the circumstances in which the police should seek CPS advice before charge

○ the need for further guidance and training in the use of the Act

○ the need to keep victims informed more effectively and support them through the pre-trial and court process.

Conclusions

● The report concludes that the use being made of the Act's criminal provisions is valid but that there is a need to clear up the confusion that exists among practitioners. This might be achieved by issuing some form of guidance or clarification from the centre about what the Act is intended to cover and through enhanced training for all practitioners, as and when opportunities arise.

● In reviewing the effectiveness of the Act, the report notes that the key components are that:

○ the police should pursue appropriate action at the right time

○ victims should be aware of the remedies available to them

○ there should be a rigorous approach to the prosecution of offenders

○ appropriate sentences are passed and executed.

The report draws attention to the need for improvements in each of these areas. Thus:

● for the police, there is a need to be clear about what can be taken to constitute a course of harassment, what proof is required and how best to proceed with a case. The need for training noted above may partly address these issues, but there is also a need to re-examine practices in collecting evidence and in seeking CPS advice;

● in terms of information for victims, there may be a need for greater publicity about the remedies for harassment contained in the Act;

- the high attrition rate of harassment cases points towards the need for greater support for victims during the pre-trial and trial process. But another implication is that only cases suitable for criminal prosecution should be filtered into the criminal process by the police in the first place;

- the operation of restraining orders – effectively the teeth of the Act – needs to be carefully examined. It is surprising that they are not invariably used in harassment convictions. But, more importantly, where they are used they should be framed in a way which is likely to maximise their effectiveness, victims should be aware of the orders and what to do if they are breached, and there should be an effective police and court response to breaches.

Introduction

Background to the research

This report examines the use and effectiveness of the Protection from Harassment Act 1997. One of the aims underlying the introduction of the Act was to tackle the problem of what is commonly referred to as stalking. Stalking has been variously defined as:

> *"wilful, malicious and repeated following and harassment of another person that threatens his or her safety" Meloy and Gothard 1995*

and as:

> *"a course of conduct directed at a specific person that involves repeated physical or visual proximity, non-consensual communication or verbal, written or implied threats" Tjaden, P. 1997*

Public perceptions of stalking have been coloured by the media attention given to high profile cases involving public figures or personalities. The victims have included members of the royal family as well as various celebrities and television presenters. However, 'repetitive, unwanted attention, communications or approaches' (Farnham et al, 2000) are by no means only perpetrated by those targeting celebrities and famous personalities. Sometimes the victims are members of the public: the case of R v Burstow[1] (see Appendix 2), for example, received considerable publicity and it was in the wake of this case that the government decided to frame legislation to address the problem.

The kinds of case which have attracted media attention, involving obsessive following and harassment of an individual, form one end of a spectrum of behaviour which might be classed more broadly as harassment that causes considerable distress to a wider constituency. Therefore, whilst one aim of the Protection from Harassment Act was to deal with stalking, the Act is wide-ranging and addresses any type of conduct amounting to 'harassment' (the term 'stalking' is not actually used in the Act). Viewed in these broader terms, harassment might include the kind of behaviour which is popularly considered to constitute stalking, but also extend to unwanted telephone calls, letters or gifts, vandalism of

---

1   This case involved victim Tracey Morgan whose experience was publicised in a television documentary: "I'll Be Watching You' (Yorkshire Television August 1999).

property or harassment of family and friends. Such behaviour may be accompanied by credible threats of violence and may, indeed, be a precursor to more serious offences (such as rape or murder).

The kind of behaviour encompassed by the Act is not necessarily associated with the unwelcome attentions of strangers (or people with mental illnesses). As will be shown and as previous research has pointed out (Farnham et al, 2000), the unwanted attentions of ex-partners and others known to the victim may also be the cause of considerable distress. Meloy (1999) has suggested that victims of harassment are most often women who have had a prior sexual or intimate relationship with the perpetrator. Tjaden (1997) has pointed to the link between harassment and "controlling behaviour and physical, emotional and sexual abuse perpetrated against women by intimate partners".

Problems with the existing law

Before the implementation of the Protection from Harassment Act, the criminal law relating to stalking in particular and harassment generally was inadequate in a number of respects:

- there was little protection for victims who were upset and frightened by a series of disturbing incidents, where the behaviour in question nonetheless fell short of being illegal

- intention to cause harassment, alarm or distress had to be proved in order to secure an adequate penalty. Thus, under section 4A of the Public Order Act 1986, there is an offence of intentionally causing harassment alarm or distress with a penalty of up to six months imprisonment. However, the requirement to prove intent on the part of the perpetrator can create difficulties. A lesser offence exists in the form of section 5 of the same Act (the offence of causing harassment alarm or distress). This does not require intent but penalties are limited.

The Protection from Harassment Act 1997

The Protection from Harassment Act came into force on June 16 1997.[2] The Act offers greater protection than the previous law in several ways: there is no requirement to prove intent but the penalties are considerable; and, through the restraining order, criminal courts can offer the equivalent of civil court injunctions.

Offences

Section 1 of the Act introduces a prohibition on any course of conduct pursued by a person which amounts to harassment of another and which he knows or ought to know amounts to such harassment. The Act then goes on to provide for two offences of harassment – a lower level (section 2) and higher level (section 4) offence.[3] In both cases harassment must be proved, with the added requirement for section 4 that the conduct caused the victim to fear, on at least two occasions, that violence would be used against him or her.

Section 2 criminal harassment is a summary offence (i.e. triable only in the magistrates' court). It carries a possible sentence of up to six months imprisonment and/or a fine of up to £5,000. The police are given the power to arrest without warrant anyone reasonably suspected of committing a section 2 offence. In short, the essential elements of the offence are that the accused must pursue a course of conduct, this must amount to harassment of another person and the accused must know, or ought to know, that the course of conduct amounts to harassment. In the event of a conviction the court can impose a restraining order prohibiting specified forms of behaviour, breach of which carries a potential sentence of up to five years imprisonment.

Section 4 is a higher level offence triable in either magistrates' courts or the Crown Court. It is punishable in the magistrates' court with up to six months imprisonment and/or a £5,000 fine and/or a restraining order; in the Crown Court the penalties are up to five years imprisonment, an unlimited fine and/or a restraining order.

For an offence of harassment to be made out, there must be a *course of conduct*, which is defined in s.7(3) as meaning 'conduct on at least two occasions'. The conduct on each

---

2   The full text of the Act is reproduced at Appendix 1.
3   Racially aggravated versions of both offences were introduced on 30 September 1998 by the Crime and Disorder Act 1998. These offences were not dealt with in the present study, although statistics about the frequency of proceedings are provided in Appendix 3.

occasion need not be the same but must contribute to the alleged course of harassment.. The Act does not specify what period of time must elapse between incidents for them to be treated as a course of conduct and the circumstances of each case must be taken into account. On the one hand, too long an interval (say of a year or more) might be taken to suggest that the incidents were not linked. On the other hand, too short an interval (of minutes or only a few hours) might lead to defence arguments that these were not separate incidents and not therefore part of a course of conduct.

Statutory defences

Under s1(3) it is a defence to a charge of criminal harassment for the accused to show in relation to a course of conduct:

- that it was pursued for the purpose of preventing or detecting crime

- that it was pursued under any enactment or rule of law or to comply with any condition or requirement imposed by any person under the enactment

- that in the particular circumstances the pursuit of the course of conduct was reasonable.

A person whose course of conduct is in question ought to know that it amounts to harassment of another if a reasonable person in possession of the same information would think the course of conduct amounted to harassment of another.

Restraining orders

If a defendant is convicted of an offence of harassment, the court has the power to impose a restraining order. Such orders are made for the purpose of protecting the victim from further harassment or conduct which will cause a fear of violence. Breach of a restraining order is an offence punishable by up to five years imprisonment, and the police may arrest on warrant anyone reasonably suspected as having violated the conditions of an order.[4]

---

4   Under s5(6), breach of any of the terms of a restraining order is an either-way offence punishable in a magistrates' court with up to six months imprisonment, or a £5,000 fine or both, and punishable in the Crown Court with up to five years imprisonment, or an unlimited fine or both.

The ability of the courts to impose such orders is a novel concept in criminal law and, in effect, resembles the civil remedy of an injunction. Typical conditions of restraining orders are:

- not to contact the victim

- not to visit the victim's home or place of work

- not to contact the victim's family

- to report to a police station or abide by a curfew.

Pre-existing criminal sanctions provided little scope for directly constraining the behaviour of the offender after conviction, unless a custodial sentence was given.

The civil remedy

A new civil procedure has also been introduced under section 3 of the Act. Applications can be made to the High Court or County Court under a statutory tort of harassment. The criminal and civil remedies were not necessarily intended to cover mutually exclusive types of behaviour and it is perfectly possible for victims to pursue a civil action in circumstances in which they might equally have reported the matter to the police and sought the arrest of the offender. The court can make an order to protect the victim from further harassment and that order has powers of arrest attached. Sections 3(6) to 3(9) create a new criminal offence for breach punishable by up to five years imprisonment or an unlimited fine or both.

The aims of the research

The Protection from Harassment Act has now been in force for three years. When the Act was implemented, the government gave an undertaking to evaluate its success in dealing with cases of harassment. During the initial stages, the government anticipated that the Act would be used relatively infrequently – perhaps in around 200 cases per year. In fact, it is clear that many more cases than this are being dealt with under the Act: Home Office statistics show that, in 1998, 4,300 persons were proceeded against for section 2 offences and 1,500 were proceeded against for section 4 offences. Given this level of use, it now seems appropriate to take stock of the way in which the Act is being used and of its effectiveness in dealing with the behaviour at which it was targeted.

The study addressed the following issues:

- how often the two offences are being used and the types of behaviour concerned

- how harassment cases are being dealt with by the agencies of the criminal justice system in terms of charge, prosecution action and conviction

- entencing practice, including the issuing of restraining orders and the way in which breaches of these orders are dealt with

- any problems that have arisen with the new legislation

- the effectiveness of the criminal provisions in terms of preventing further harassment and providing protection for the victim.

Methodology

The study was carried out in four criminal justice areas which had a reasonable throughput of harassment cases. In total, the research looked at a sample of 167 Protection from Harassment cases sent by the police to the Crown Prosecution Service (CPS) during 1998 for a decision on prosecution. The sample included a total of 104 section 2 and 63 section 4 cases,[5] drawn more or less equally from the four areas, representing a mixture of urban, rural and metropolitan regions. Using CPS files as the main source of information, details were recorded about the characteristics of each case and its progress through the criminal justice system.

The 167 cases involved 136 suspects, indicating that nearly a quarter of suspects in the sample were prosecuted for harassment on more than one occasion. It was intended to include an examination of charge files submitted by the police to the CPS for advice. However, no examples of such files were found and the study was not therefore able to consider this aspect of the prosecution process.

The study also drew upon Home Office statistics on court proceedings to provide information about the total number of Protection from Harassment cases proceeded with nationally and their outcome.

---

5   Nationally, the ratio of proceedings for section 2 to section 4 offences is 3:1. To take account of the difference in the proportion of s.2 and s.4 cases sampled in the research, the data were appropriately weighted when analysis was carried out on the full sample of cases.

In order to gain the perspective of the criminal justice agencies on the working of the Act, two focus groups were carried out in each of the four areas with police, prosecutors and magistrates. Respondents were selected on the basis of their familiarity in dealing with harassment cases (although, sometimes, this experience was limited). The focus groups were wide-ranging but covered a core list of topics. Practitioners were asked about their experiences of the legislation and for information about any difficulties in investigating, charging and prosecuting harassment cases.

Interviews were also carried out with 20 victims of harassment. Given that a principal aim of the Act is to provide protection for victims, respondents were asked whether they felt that this aim had been achieved. The interviews also elicited information about the different types of harassment endured and how complaints were dealt with once they had been reported to the police. All victims were drawn from the sample of 167 cases on which the statistical findings of the study are based.

Structure of the report

Chapter 2 looks at the nature of cases that are being dealt with under the Protection from Harassment Act. It considers the relationship between complainant and suspect and the sorts of behaviour which are taken to constitute harassment. Chapter 3 explores the way in which the police dealt with complaints of harassment. It examines the kind of problems encountered in the decision to charge. It also looks at steps taken to protect the victim at this stage, through the imposition of police bail conditions. Chapter 4 looks at CPS decision - making in harassment cases including the termination of cases and the use of bindovers. The chapter goes on to look at the outcome of cases in the courts, including plea, conviction, sentencing and the imposition of restraining orders. Chapter 5 reports the views of police officers, Crown Prosecutors and magistrates on the working of the Protection from Harassment Act. The conclusions of the study are presented in Chapter 6.

2   The nature of harassment cases

The findings reported in this chapter are based on the sample of 167 CPS case files and interviews with police officers and Crown Prosecutors.

Relationship between complainant and suspect

The media portrayal of stalking is of 'repetitive, unwanted attention, communications or approaches' (Farnham et al, 2000) from obsessive, psychotic strangers or fanatics.

In fact, the present study found that the kind of behaviour dealt with under the Act was linked less with strangers or people with mental illnesses than with the unwanted attentions of ex-partners and harassment by neighbours. Other research has reached a similar conclusion (Farnham et al, 2000).

Table 2.1 shows the relationship between suspect and complainant in cases examined by the study.

Table 2.1   Relationship of suspect to complainant

	%	Unweighted n=
Stranger	2	(4)
Neighbour	16	(26)
Acquaintance	41	(68)
Casually acquainted	24	(49)
Brief previous relationship	11	(13)
Work colleague	3	(6)
Intimate	41	(69)
Ex-partner	33	(54)
Relative	4	(8)
Current partner[6]	1	(1)
Friend	4	(6)
Total (unweighted n=)	100	(167)

Four main categories of case were identified:

- 'stranger' cases, where the suspect had had no contact with the complainant prior to the harassment; there were just four cases in this category

- 'neighbour' cases, where the suspect lived next door to the complainant or in the immediate vicinity

- 'acquaintance' cases, where the suspect and complainant were casually known to one another in some way

- cases involving 'intimates'. Suspects were usually ex-partners of the complainant. In eight cases the suspect was a relative.

---

6   In one case the perpetrator of the harassment was the current husband of the complainant, which was unusual since most intimate cases involved ex-partners. The behaviour constituted abuse, both verbal and physical, of the complainant over a matter concerning their daughter. The police chose to arrest the suspect under the Protection from Harassment Act.

The study showed that:

- in almost all cases the suspect and complainant were known to each other, albeit that the relationship was minimal in some cases

- in 41 per cent of cases the perpetrators were intimates of the complainant. These tended to be cases where the legislation was used to deal with situations in which there had been some kind of domestic dispute or crisis

- in 41 per cent of cases the complainants and suspects were acquaintances. They might only know each other by sight, be work colleagues or have had a previous casual relationship

- 16 per cent of cases arose from neighbour disputes. Such cases sometimes involved harassment of a single victim by several offenders from the one household (four cases) or the harassment of more than one victim by a single offender (5 cases). The remaining cases in this group involved one complainant and one offender

- in only two per cent of cases (involving 4 suspects) were the parties strangers. The complainants in these cases were all female. Interviews with practitioners confirmed that such cases, which typically involve classic 'stalking' behaviour, were few and far between.

Eighty per cent of suspects in the sample were male and 79 per cent of victims were female. Table 2.2 shows that suspects in cases involving intimates were even more likely to be males.

Table 2.2   Gender of suspect by complainant / suspect relationship

	Strangers %	Acquaintances %	Neighbours %	Intimates %	All cases %
Male	50	67	68	94	80
Female	50	33	32	6	20
Total (unweighted n=)	4	68	26	69	167

Anecdotal evidence from interviewees suggests that the kinds of relationships between complainants and suspects picked up by the study may not be the only ones which exist in harassment cases. In particular, it was suggested that the Act is sometimes used to deal with harassment arising in relation to picketing during the course of industrial disputes and animal rights and other protests.

Behaviour

Table 2.3 lists the types of behaviour which the police treated as harassment in cases in the sample.

Table 2.3   The nature of harassment

	All cases %
Threats	
Face-to-face verbal harassment	60
Threatening phone calls/letters/gifts	49
Distressing behaviour	
Following	15
Standing/parked outside	49
Harassment of family	37
Non-violent physical harassment[7]	14
Silent phone calls	13
Obscene phone calls	3
'Nice' letters/gifts	16
Damage to property	38
Violent behaviour	15
Other behaviour	21
Total (unweighted n=)	167

Note: percentages sum to more than 100 because there was often more than one type of harassment in each case.

Almost all cases involved more than a single form of harassment. It was very rare for there to be just one type of behaviour.

The types of behaviour found in the present study are perhaps best illustrated using case studies.

---

7   Physical harassment can include unwanted displays of affection, which do not actually cause injury and can be differentiated from violent behaviour.

Intimates

Intimate cases were most often characterised by behaviour that was both intimidating and distressing in nature. This sometimes involved verbal threats or entailed more innocuous acts which might be pleasant under other circumstances but caused distress in these instances.

Case study 1

This case involved a victim and an offender who had been involved in a three-year relationship.

Prior to the Protection from Harassment Act, the victim had endured a history of domestic violence which had been dealt with by police through arrest for assault or breach of the peace. The offender's aggressive behaviour was ultimately the catalyst for the breakdown of the relationship.

On one occasion, the offender would not leave when the victim asked him to and he caused an incident to which the police were called. He was warned that his behaviour constituted a breach of the peace and, at the request of the victim, was asked to leave the premises.

Following this, the offender embarked on a course of behaviour which caused both distress and embarrassment to the victim. Behaviour at first was quite aggressive: he was seen on several occasions outside her home shouting abuse and threats and demanding to see her. She also received threatening as well as obscene letters and silent telephone calls. The offender also physically assaulted the victim one day when she was out with a friend. She returned home to find damage to her property where he had tried to gain entry into the house as well as graffiti on her front door. Behaviour then turned to a more 'pleasant' form of contact, where the offender sent letters and made telephone calls declaring how much he loved her and wanted her back.

Acquaintances

As with intimates, harassment in acquaintance cases often comprised behaviour that was threatening and distressing. Sometimes this affected others as well.

Case study 2

The victim worked in a hostel which offered support and resettlement services for homeless people. She was a key-worker in the hostel for the person who was to be the offender in the case. The latter had started to become very aggressive towards other residents and eventually was asked to leave the hostel.

The harassment that followed was directed at the former key-worker. The offender was very accusatory, maintaining that she had ejected him from the hostel unfairly and that he would make her pay for this. His behaviour consisted of threats in the form of letters and telephone calls, some of which were also directed at other workers in the hostel. The offender was also seen outside the hostel, where he shouted verbal abuse at the victim on several occasions and actually followed her home twice. The harassment was always threatening in nature and the victim became quite distressed and intimidated by the offender's conduct.

Neighbours

Disputes between neighbours sometimes differ from other types of harassment in that there was not always a single victim and single offender. The following case involved two victims and several offenders.

Case study 3

The victims in this instance were an elderly couple who had lived in their home for many years. A family moved into the property next door and shortly afterwards the harassment started.

The victims endured a constant barrage of noise pollution in the form of loud music and much shouting. The male victim complained to the neighbours, asking that they keep the noise down in respect for other residents. As a result of this, the offenders took an instant dislike to the couple and the father, in particular, embarked on a course of harassment. This involved verbal abuse, defacing their front door and putting rubbish through the letter-box. Whenever the victims left the house they were subject to obscene language and were often followed by one or more of the offenders. Occasionally, objects would be thrown at the house or into their garden and at one point paint was thrown over their car.

Strangers

There were too few stranger cases for any comprehensive pattern to be discerned. However, of the cases that were included in the present study, the sort of harassment noted in the following two examples was distinctly intimidating. The behaviour concerned made the victims feel uneasy and perhaps unsure about what to expect.

Case study 4

The victim lived in a flat which was part of a communal residence. She had been aware for a few days of a man who sat on the stairs near to her flat and made obscene threats when she walked past, behaviour which she found quite distressing.

One day, she was returning home with her daughter. On entering the public area she was conscious of the man's presence as he followed her up the stairs. He was shouting at her and threatening to harm her and her child. She became quite intimidated by his behaviour and entered her flat quickly. The offender tried to push the door open but she managed to close and lock it, fearing for her safety. He continued to shout threats, using obscene language, and to kick her door. The police were called and the offender was arrested. He was charged with a section 4 offence.

(The offender in this case was found to be mentally disordered and his case was later dropped.)

Case study 5

The victim worked in a shop. A man came into the shop on several occasions and stared at the victim in a manner which made her feel uncomfortable. He sometimes approached her and made obscene suggestions. He never bought anything. He was also seen standing outside the shop looking in on several occasions and the behaviour was always the same. The manager of the shop was aware of the man but felt unable to do anything since he had not apparently committed an offence.

One time, the victim met the offender in the street and he pinched her bottom as he walked past. Again, she felt humiliated and distressed by his behaviour. A plain-clothes police officer attended the shop and was witness to the offender's intimidating behaviour. The police officer proceeded to arrest the man who tried to assault him. He was later charged with a section 2 offence.

Reasons for harassment

Table 2.4 shows the main reasons why harassment occurred, in as much as they could be discerned from the information on file.

Table 2.4   Principal reasons for harassment

	Acquaintances %	Intimates %	Neighbours %	Strangers %	All %
Complainant ended relationship	23	83	–	–	43
Disputes over property/money	2	–	86	–	14
Personal dispute	51	10	–	–	25
Business dispute	6	–	–	–	3
No apparent reason	–	–	–	80	2
Mentally disordered suspect	9	2	6	20	7
Suspect is in love with complainant	7	–	–	–	3
Issues regarding access to children	–	5	–	–	2
Racially motivated	1	–	8	–	2
Total (unweighted n=)	64	68	22	3	157

Notes:
1.   n=157. Information on reasons for harassment and complainant/suspect relationship was missing in ten cases.
2.   percentages do not always sum to 100 due to rounding.

- The most common reason for harassment was that the complainant had decided to terminate a relationship with the suspect – this was the reported reason in over 80 per cent of cases involving intimates and in 43 per cent of cases overall. The harassment appeared to be symptomatic of the suspect not coming to terms with the situation.

- Harassment among neighbours most often arose from disputes relating to property or money, or from jealousy.

- A few cases involved mentally disordered suspects, where there appeared to be no other apparent motive for the harassment than the suspect's particular obsession or fixation.

- Harassment apparently precipitated by some form of racial motivation was rare – just three cases were recorded, two of which fell into the category of neighbour disputes.

3   Police action in harassment cases

Reporting to the police

Most complainants interviewed were not aware of the Protection from Harassment Act or of what to expect prior to their reporting incidents of harassment to the police. About half of those interviewed had endured the unwanted behaviour for a significant period before they decided to report it, perhaps reflecting the fact that most do not realise that the behaviour to which they were subjected might now be an offence. Information for victims of harassment is sparse in contrast, for example, to information about the services available for victims of domestic violence.

Complainants usually chose the police as their first point of contact when making a complaint. The response from some victims interviewed was not necessarily positive:

> "The police weren't unsympathetic, I just felt a nuisance...when I really did cry about it because it had become too much...only then...did they realise that something definitely had to be done about him."
>
> Victim

Interviews with the police revealed that complainants were sometimes directed to them via a solicitor, especially in cases involving neighbour disputes. A further source of information might be the media: certainly the television soap 'The Bill' was mentioned by some police officers as one programme that had addressed the issue of harassment.

Course of conduct

The offences established by the Protection from Harassment Act require that a 'course of conduct' ('conduct on at least two occasions' – s7(3)) should have occurred, rather than a single incident. This can include previously unreported incidents (as long as they occurred after the implementation of the Protection from Harassment Act). Once a first incident of harassment has been identified, the police must wait for a further incident or incidents before an offence under the Act may be considered. The police then have the power to arrest the suspect. More commonly the course of conduct will include incidents previously reported to the police, where a record of action taken might be available.

- In one-third of cases, a suspect was arrested on the third occasion that a complaint was made. In a few cases the police waited until the fourth, fifth or even in one case the eighth complaint.

- Contrary to the requirements of the legislation, the police occasionally arrested suspects where there had been a single incident. This occurred in ten per cent of cases. It is, of course, possible that earlier incidents were poorly recorded and did not show up in police records. Two of the cases involved harassment by strangers and violence. These cases may have been seen as more serious in nature and requiring immediate action.

- Nearly two-thirds of suspects had been warned on a previous occasion about their behaviour prior to being arrested.

- In ten cases, incidents forming part of the alleged course of conduct had previously been dealt with by way of charge for offences such as theft, criminal damage or threats to kill. In these cases, suspects were usually arrested after the third incident since the initial incident could not count towards the overall course of conduct.

In the majority of cases, the harassment reported was carried out relatively frequently. Thus, 42 per cent of complainants reported that they had been subject to an incident every few days and 22 per cent at least once a day and often more frequently.

The fact that the police must wait to prove a course of conduct runs the risk that action might not be taken early enough to prevent harm to the victim. However, there are steps which the police can take at an early stage. For instance, an incident might be dealt with by way of an informal warning – something that, in itself, might alarm the perpetrator enough to cease their behaviour.

In order to prove a course of conduct, it is important that the police do not deal with an initial incident by way of charge or a formal caution. As noted above, doing so will render that incident null and void for the purposes of it being taken into account as part of a course of behaviour. It is important that officers are aware of this requirement from training in the use of the Act, otherwise there is the danger that cases will be dropped because the elements of the offence have not been made out. Interviews with officers certainly revealed some confusion over the issue.

The police interviews also pointed to other uncertainties in this area: for example, over how many warnings should be given before there was the power to arrest. The length of time that must elapse between incidents before they can be counted separately also caused some confusion. At one end of the scale, the longer the time between incidents the less likely they are to be treated as constituting a course of conduct. At the other extreme, two incidents separated by, say, ten minutes would also be unlikely to be counted as a course of behaviour. Decisions are often subjective. Needless to say, defence lawyers would do their best to argue that incidents close together in time did not constitute a course of conduct.

Evidence

"You have to gain your own evidence to prove a) to yourself that you're not going mad and b) to the legal system that he's here, look at what he's doing."

Tracey Morgan

In order to make out a case of harassment, various points need to be proven. As mentioned, a course of conduct must be established. It must also be shown that the offender knew or ought to have known that their behaviour amounts to harassment of another or, in the case of a section 4 offence, caused a fear of violence. There are a number of difficulties in providing such proof. One is that what may appear to some – including perhaps the perpetrator – as harmless behaviour may well be perceived differently by the victim. To an extent, the test is both objective and subjective, in that it must be proved that the perpetrator knew or ought to have known what effect his or her behaviour might have but also that the behaviour in fact caused harassment to the particular victim. Another difficulty is that very often there is no corroborating evidence and that most cases come down to the victim's word against that of the perpetrator. As a result, the collection of any available evidence is vital and the police must ensure that this is done methodically and as early as possible.

"It would have been far easier if he had just come and raped me or murdered me because then it would be over with."

Tracey Morgan

In harassment cases, it is clear that the police must make a note of each incident. They might even consider directing the victim to a solicitor and action such as this would provide important confirmation that an incident had occurred. A difficulty arises where different officers deal with incidents involving the same parties without being aware that the police have previously been called to similar incidents. It is therefore important that records are made and stored in a way that makes them easily accessible. Prior police warnings may provide useful evidence of a course of conduct, especially if there is supporting evidence in the form of a letter of warning.

Notes were usually made in officers' pocket books at the time that warnings were issued and in some instances would be recorded on the Police National Computer (PNC). However, this was not the case in all forces, and the recording of warnings was sometimes sketchy. As a result officers called to incidents might often be unaware of the previous history of relations between the complainant and the suspect.

Table 3.1 shows the main sources of evidence (apart from evidence from victims themselves) which were available in cases in the sample.

Table 3.1   Evidence available against the suspect

Category of evidence	All cases %
Independent eye witness	75
Documentary evidence	50
Material/forensic	46
Full confession	25
Police eye witness	20
Medical	5
Circumstantial	5
Other evidence	3
Total (unweighted n=)	167

Notes:
1. n=167 cases.
2. Percentages sum to more than 100 because more than one type of evidence was often available per case.

- *Eye witness evidence*
  Independent eye witnesses were the most important source of evidence in three-quarters of cases in the study. Police eye witnesses were also an important source of corroboratory evidence in 20 per cent of cases.

- *Documentary evidence*
  Complainants are usually advised by the police to keep a diary of the behaviour and to log incidents, recording dates, times and places. Such

documents provided important evidence in a half of cases, usually involving unwanted telephone calls.

- *Material or forensic evidence*
  In nearly half of cases there was some form of forensic or material evidence, for example in the form of letters or photographs.

- *Full confession*
  In a quarter of cases, the suspect made a full confession.

- *Medical evidence*
  Doctors' reports might be drawn upon to reveal the psychological stresses and strains on the victim as a result of the harassment. They might also point to evidence of physical injury. However, in cases in which the harm is of a serious physical nature it is likely that assault charges would have been brought rather than a harassment charge.

In addition, police officers also mentioned the following as sometimes being important sources of evidence:

- *Prior police warnings*
  These may provide useful evidence of a course of conduct, especially if there is supporting evidence in the form of a letter of warning.

- *Telephone bills*
  In the event of unwanted telephone calls, contact is often made with British Telecom for itemised bills for the alleged perpetrator's telephone number.

- *Evidence from other agencies*
  In the event of neighbour disagreements, action is often taken in partnership with council environmental health services or housing association bodies, whose statements may provide valuable supporting evidence.

CPS advice

The police have the option of seeking CPS advice before charging a suspect if, for example, they are unsure about whether the evidence is sufficient or about the nature of the charges they should bring (Crisp and Moxon, 1994).

Despite the evidential problems noted above in relation to harassment cases, no cases in the study were referred to the CPS for advice. Some of the police officers interviewed maintained that harassment cases are not usually particularly complicated and therefore do not warrant approaching the CPS for advice prior to a decision to charge. However, others appreciated the benefit of more informal liaison between the police and CPS, and perhaps even joint training, to enhance mutual understanding of the guidelines that each are working to in such cases.

In more difficult cases, where advice was required, it tended to be sought from senior colleagues. Some scepticism about the CPS amongst the police caused them to feel that submitting advice files would invariably invite suggestions of no further action. They therefore preferred to press ahead and to let the CPS see the case once they had gathered all the evidence they considered necessary.

Police charges

In 1998, national statistics show that 4,300 persons were proceeded against for section 2 offences and 1,500 for the more serious section 4 offence.

Interviews revealed that one factor entering into police officers' thinking in deciding on the most appropriate charge was the perception that the section 2 (less serious) offence would be "easier to run with". In contrast to section 4, it was not necessary to prove that the harassment caused the victim to fear that violence would be used against him or her on at least two occasions. Ultimately, however, the decision on what to charge was primarily guided by the gravity of the alleged victim's complaint. In the case of section 4 offences, the choice of a harassment charge in preference to certain other offences, such as assault, was often influenced by the consideration that a conviction under the Act could result in a more serious custodial sentence and gave access to the remedy of a restraining order (see Chapter 4).

However, not all officers were aware of the difference between section 2 and section 4 offences and the choice between one and the other was not therefore always an informed one. This raises the issue of the level of training which officers had received on the Act. The Home Office has attempted to provide training to a limited number of officers in each force, in the hope that they would cascade this information down to the officer on the beat. It is perhaps not surprising, given the other demands on officers, that this did not always happen. At junior levels, therefore, officers often did not have good knowledge of the Act or how it should be used. One suggestion for improving on this situation was that a national document should be issued which would explain the scope and purpose of the Act and how the police should deal with harassment cases.[8] This could be developed and distributed force-wide. Another suggestion was for an expert to be trained in the Protection from Harassment Act in each force, to whom officers could refer:

"It needs somebody to explain to every bobby who's on the beat what we can do with this law and how it works."

Police training officer

Police bail

After charge, the police have to give careful consideration to the question of bail, since the suspect's release may result in a resumption of the offending behaviour. Perhaps the best form of protection that the police can offer a victim of harassment is to remand the suspect in custody after charge. This occurred in seven per cent of cases. Where the suspect was bailed after charge and pending first court appearance, the police usually imposed bail conditions with the aim of keeping the alleged offender away from the complainant. To this end, nearly 90 per cent of those who were bailed received bail conditions.

- Sixty-eight per cent of those given bail conditions were required not to contact the victim and 57 per cent were required not to contact any witnesses in the case.

- Thirty-five per cent were ordered to keep away from the victim's address and 51 per cent from any place in which the victim was likely to be.

- In 21 per cent of cases the alleged offender was required to reside at a specific address.

---

8   A Home Office document is due to be published in 2000 which provides guidance for investigators on how to deal with harassment cases. It is intended that this be distributed force-wide.

Magistrates maintained that perpetrators of harassment are susceptible to breaching bail conditions, especially in cases involving intimates. They expressed some concern that suspects are re-bailed too readily in the event of breaches.

There are other forms of protection that the police can offer although, because of their resource implications, these are mainly used in more serious cases where there is a real risk of harm. During interviews, the police mentioned the possibility of installing panic buttons, alarms or giving out emergency numbers. However, in cases at the serious end of the spectrum suspects would usually be remanded in custody.

Keeping the victim informed

Harassment affects victims' lives considerably and as a result there is a very real need for them to know what is happening in their case and whether there is any prospect of the harassment resuming.

> "Your whole life revolves around 'is he going to get out today, I want to know, I need to know because I don't just want to go out the door and see him there."
>
> Victim

> "Because of the nature of this harassment, I think you personally feel obliged to keep them informed, you know."
>
> Police officer

> "It is the be all and end all to them, it is the biggest concern in their life at the moment, really they like to know that they have been dealt with."
>
> Police officer

Interviews with complainants revealed that they were generally aware of what was happening in their cases since the police often had occasion to contact them during the course of the investigation. As a result, the police often tended to build up a rapport with complainants. However, a few police officers maintained that they are in touch with a complainant up to the point of arrest and charge, but that there is sometimes a problem thereafter since they themselves are not always aware of what is going on in specific cases. This can result in numerous contacts from complainants asking for information:

"The minute they get your name and your phone number, they will stick to you like glue and they will be on the phone every two minutes."

[Police officer]

Although the police sometimes found the degree of contact with complainants irksome, they accepted that they were probably best placed to provide them with the information they needed. Some victims also raised the problem of there being one officer dealing with the case and in the event of the officer being off duty nobody else would be able to deal with any complaints.

"If anything happens within that time, [the victim] calls police officers who don't know what the case is all about or what's happened and so you have to go over it all again or wait for the officer to come back. Where does that leave the victim?"

Victim

These problems of communication lay at the heart of the One Stop Shop initiative, under which victims were able to receive information about the progress of their case from a single source (Hoyle C et al. 1998). However, although the initiative has been piloted, it has not as yet been adopted in a uniform way nationally.

It was argued by some practitioners and, indeed, victims that increased support for victims of harassment would also be useful. At present, the referral of victims to Victim Support in harassment cases is not mandatory and there might be an argument to make it so. This could provide the victim with information about what they can expect to happen and any necessary counselling, since the police are more concerned with investigating the case.

"I suppose, like teachers, police officers aren't counsellors, they deal with your case. But, you do wish that you sometimes had some sort of moral support."

Victim

4   The prosecution process and court proceedings

CPS decision-making

This chapter looks at the way in which cases are dealt with by the CPS and courts. The findings are based on the sample of 167 cases as well as interviews with practitioners.

Once the police have charged a suspect, the case is submitted to the CPS, who must review the case and decide whether to proceed with a prosecution. In reaching their decision, CPS lawyers apply the evidential and public interest tests set out in the Code for Crown Prosecutors. First, they must decide whether there is a 'realistic prospect of conviction'. If there is insufficient evidence, the case is discontinued. Second, if the evidence is sufficient, the CPS must decide whether it is in the public interest to proceed. Among the public interest factors which might be considered as favouring prosecution are: violence or a weapon was used during the commission of the offence; the victim was vulnerable, was put in considerable fear, or suffered personal attack, damage or disturbance; or that the offence was motivated by any form of discrimination against the victim's ethnic origin or gender. On the other hand, some factors might be taken to count against prosecution. These could include the likelihood that the court would impose a nominal penalty, prosecution is likely to have a very bad effect on the victim's physical or mental health or the defendant is elderly or is suffering from significant mental or physical ill health (CPS, 1994).

Table 4.1 shows what happened to suspects whose cases were referred to the CPS for a decision on prosecution. The cases against 39 per cent were dropped. The likelihood of termination varied according to the relationship between complainant and suspect. No cases involving 'strangers' were dropped, compared with nearly half of those classified as 'neighbour' cases and 41 per cent of those involving 'intimates'.

Almost all terminations were on grounds of insufficient evidence. Evidential reasons were particularly likely to be cited in 'neighbour' cases where there were often counter-allegations and ultimately the case rested on the complainant's word against that of the suspect. In many such cases the CPS sought a bindover in return for dropping proceedings (see below).

Table 4.1   Complainant/suspect relationship and CPS decision

	Strangers %	Acquaintances %	Neighbours %	Intimates %	Total %
Terminated	–	38	46	41	39
Proceeded with	100	62	54	59	61
Total (unweighted n=)	4	66	26	71	167

Note:
1. unweighted n=167 (cases for which complainant/suspect relationship and CPS decision were known)

The termination rate varied slightly according to the charge although the difference was not statistically significant: 42 per cent of section 2 cases were dropped compared with 38 per cent of section 4 cases.

The termination rate for harassment cases of 39 per cent appears high when compared with the national average for all cases of 14 per cent. However, a high termination rate tends to be associated with cases in which the parties are known to each other. Rape and domestic violence are two notable examples where a high number of cases are also dropped (Grace et al, 1995; Harris and Grace, 1999). Where the complainant does not wish to proceed, as often happens in these cases, there is often little in the way of independent evidence.

In the present study, complainants not wishing to proceed were responsible for one-third of terminations. Such cases were most likely to involve intimates. Sixty-three per cent of cases where the complainant did not wish to proceed involved an ex-partner.

Officers interviewed flagged up complainants not wanting to proceed as a particularly frustrating problem for them. Some even suggested that it might make the police more reluctant to intervene in harassment cases in the future:

"I mean, sometimes you wonder why bother – 24 hours later they're back in love and don't want to make a formal complaint."

Police officer

One magistrate also drew attention to the fact that harassment cases must be handled with some degree of caution, maintaining that some accusations will be mistaken or even vindictive:

"It's the easiest thing in the world…for a woman to make an accusation against a man".

Magistrate

Bindovers

A bindover can be sought where a trial does not seem appropriate or where the evidence is unlikely to support a conviction and the defendant agrees to the conditions imposed. For example, where complainants are unwilling to give evidence in court, a bindover will still offer some form of protection. Technically, such cases are treated as terminations, since the CPS will usually offer no evidence in return for the court agreeing to a bindover. The alleged offenders are warned that if they breach the order they will fall to be dealt with for that matter as well as any subsequent offences.

- In 47 per cent of cases discontinued, the CPS successfully sought a bindover without a trial. This occurred in 57 per cent of cases involving neighbours, 33 per cent involving intimates and 27 per cent involving acquaintances.

CPS lawyers generally stressed that they would not like to see the option of a bindover taken away. In contrast, some magistrates felt that bindovers were potentially a recipe for disaster, and that harassment would almost certainly not be prevented in this way. It was seen as:

"[making] it look like we've done something ...... a pretty toothless disposal".

Magistrate

Just over three-quarters of bindovers were imposed for 12 months and were usually in the region of £100.

Mental disorder

In a few cases – six per cent of those terminated - proceedings were discontinued on the basis that the suspect was mentally disordered and that it was not in the public interest to proceed with a prosecution. These were all cases involving acquaintances.

Cases where there is a mentally disordered suspect can pose problems in any criminal investigation in terms of the most effective way of proceeding. Some officers interviewed expressed frustration that, where the alleged offender was suspected to be suffering from a mental disorder, the result was likely to be that the CPS would drop the case. The effect of early diversion away from the criminal justice system was to deprive the victim of the remedy of a restraining order, which is only available by securing a criminal conviction in the courts. One victim was concerned that the issue of the mental health of the offender had been brought up in their case:

"For me the frustrating thing is he is bright enough and articulate enough...to wilfully know that he can simply stop taking [his medication], go into overdrive, go and harass somebody and then slip back under the convenient cover of his 'illness'."

Victim

In the present study, cases involving suspects who were believed to be mentally disordered were relatively rare. In 14 per cent of cases the police carried out some investigation into the suspect's psychiatric history. However, no suspects in the study underwent psychiatric assessment by a doctor and the police maintained that this very rarely happened. From interviews with the police and CPS, it seems that, in the rare cases where psychiatric assessment is undertaken, the result is invariably a finding of a personality disorder which is untreatable. Other work by Farnham, et al. (2000) has drawn attention to the fact that the greatest danger of serious violence from a stalker in the United Kingdom is not from strangers or people with a psychotic illness but from non-psychotic ex-partners. This helps to explain why most suspects do not undergo any form of psychiatric assessment.

Tracey Morgan, herself a victim of stalking, is instrumental in a campaign, in consultation with the Suzy Lamplugh Trust, advising that all suspects arrested under the Protection from Harassment Act undergo psychiatric assessment.

"I think it's a good law but it doesn't actually deal with the problem. He has a personality disorder, he's not going to stop."

Tracey Morgan

Police who were interviewed maintained that this would not be wise since the great majority of people arrested under the Act do not appear to have a mental disorder, although some might experience some mental trauma in the short term due, say, to a relationship breakdown. It was felt that labelling these suspects as possibly mentally disordered by referring them for psychiatric assessment would not be very helpful, and would be very costly. However, the suggestion may have been made with the archetypal fixated stalker in mind and, as the present study indicates, most Protection from Harassment offenders do not fall into this category.

Court bail

The CPS sought and obtained court bail with conditions in just over three-quarters of cases proceeded with which were not completed at first court appearance. Ten per cent of defendants were held in custody following their first court appearance.

CPS lawyers emphasised the importance of bail conditions in harassment cases as the primary need is usually to keep the alleged offender away from the complainant. The nature of the conditions imposed illustrate this.

- In 61 per cent of cases where conditions were imposed, the accused was instructed not to contact the victim or any witnesses in the case, and in a further 33 per cent the defendant was forbidden to go to the complainant's home

- In 59 per cent of conditions cases, the accused was required to report to the police on a regular basis. This condition was particularly likely to be imposed in cases involving intimates (in three-quarters of such cases)

- In 51 per cent of cases where conditions were imposed, the accused was prohibited from going near a specified place

- In 32 per cent of cases a curfew was placed upon the accused, requiring him or her to stay indoors between specified hours; such a requirement was especially likely to be imposed in neighbour dispute cases.

Breaches of bail

In 21 per cent of cases in which conditions were imposed, suspects were known to have breached their bail conditions. By way of comparison with cases generally, a recent study in two police areas found that nine per cent of defendants bailed by the court were known to have breached their conditions (Brown, 1998).

Magistrates alleged that perpetrators of harassment are particularly susceptible to breaching bail conditions. In particular, because they may have been involved in a course of conduct for some while, it might be difficult for them simply to cease the behaviour. Just over a half of breaches in the present study occurred in cases involving 'intimates'. Some practitioners, particularly the CPS, also maintained that magistrates have a tendency to re-bail alleged offenders, even after breaches of conditions, and argued that this was not a very satisfactory state of affairs. Breaches were usually dealt with by changing the conditions of the bail agreement.

Charge amendment

Where the CPS decided to proceed with a prosecution, it was not always on the same charges as those laid by the police. Thus, four per cent of those charged with section 2 offences faced a section 4 charge at court and four per cent some other charge. And, of those charged under section 4, the charge was reduced to section 2 in nine per cent of cases and altered to some other charge in a further 13 per cent of cases.

Outcome at court

Table 4.2   Magistrates' court outcome – all cases proceeding to a hearing.

	All cases %	Unweighted (n=)
Guilty plea	63	56
Conviction following contest	18	19
Dismissed	16	16
Committed for trial	3	3
Total (unweighted n=)	100	94

Notes:
1.   unweighted n=94 (in 8 cases information on outcome was missing).
2.   the figure for conviction following contest includes 8 per cent of cases in which defendants were bound over after trial.
3.   the 16 per cent of cases dismissed include those acquitted following a trial and those dismissed no case to answer.

- In 63 per cent of cases the defendant pleaded guilty

- Eighteen per cent of cases resulted in a conviction following a contest

- Sixteen per cent of cases were dismissed either following trial or because the magistrates accepted that there was no case to answer

- Three section 4 cases were committed to the Crown Court for trial:

    - types of behaviour here included violent threats and threats to kill

    - two were convicted of both principal and other charges, whilst one was convicted of an alternative charge.

Convictions

The conviction rate in cases going to a hearing was 84 per cent.

Section 2 and section 4 cases were almost equally likely to result in conviction. However, defendants facing a section 2 charge were more likely to be convicted of that charge than were those facing a section 4 charge:

- Ninety-six per cent of those who faced a section 2 charge at court were convicted of that charge

- Sixty-six per cent of those facing a section 4 charge were convicted of that charge; a further 19 per cent were convicted of a section 2 offence; the remainder were convicted of some other offence (such as assault or criminal damage).

Twelve per cent of defendants were convicted of other offences in addition to the principal section 2 or section 4 charge. These included assault, criminal damage and offences under the Telecommunications Act.

No suspects were given formal cautions for offences under the Act.

Defences

Under s1(3) it is a defence to a charge of criminal harassment for the accused to show in relation to a course of conduct:

a)   that it was pursued for the purpose of preventing or detecting crime

b)   that it was pursued under any enactment or rule of law or to comply with any condition or requirement imposed by any person under the enactment

c)   that in the particular circumstances the pursuit of the course of conduct was reasonable.

A person whose course of conduct is in question ought to know that it amounts to harassment of another if a reasonable person in possession of the same information would think the course of conduct amounted to harassment of another."

Relatively little information was available about the defences which were put forward at court. Where it was known what defence was put forward, nearly half of defendants argued that their behaviour had been reasonable and the remainder offered some other explanation for their actions.

In 16 section 4 cases the issue of possible mental disorder was raised, although this is not a statutory defence. Ten of these cases involved intimates. Most of these went to a hearing rather than being discontinued and three - quarters resulted in a conviction and sentence.

Sentence

Table 4.3 shows the sentences given to those convicted of harassment, as well as for other offences where the initial charge had been one of harassment.

Table 4.3   Principal sentence by offence

	PFHA (Section 2) %	PFHA (Section 4) %	Other conviction %	All cases %
Bound over	12	46	12	16
Conditional discharge	37	46	77	43
Fine	14	–	–	10
Compensation order	2	–	–	2
Community sentence	32		12	25
Imprisonment	4	8	–	3
total (unweighted n=)	48	11	15	74

Notes:
1.   unweighted n=74 (in 4 cases information was missing).
2.   'community sentence' includes: probation order with/without requirements, community service order, attendance centre order and combination order.
3.   percentages may not sum to 100 due to rounding.

- The sentence most frequently awarded (in 43% of convictions) was a conditional discharge.

- A quarter received community sentences.

Restraining orders

"The complainants in these cases.... they are not bothered about what the punishment is going to be, they just want it to stop and if we can achieve that, then we have achieved something."

Police officer

If a defendant is convicted of an offence of harassment, the court has the power to impose a restraining order. Such orders are made:

"...for the purpose of protecting the victim of the offence, or any other person mentioned in the order, from further conduct which –

a) amounts to harassment; or

b) will cause a fear of violence..." (s.5(2) PFH Act).

The granting of a restraining order depends on the court accepting the conditions proposed by the prosecution. While restraining orders fall within the sentencing powers of the court, magistrates or judges will usually expect prosecutors to suggest what conditions might be appropriate. Restraining orders were usually granted where requested, but in ten per cent of cases, and particularly in those concerning neighbour disputes, the court declined to issue them.

- Restraining orders were issued in 56 per cent of cases in which there was a conviction; the rate at which they were issued varied slightly according to the type of case, although these findings were not statistically significant.

- Restraining orders were most frequently issued in conjunction with a conditional discharge – 79 per cent.

- Restraining orders were usually specified to run for 12 or 18 months, although in five cases (four involved intimates) the order was made to run until further notice.

Table 4.4   Conditions of restraining orders

	Cases %
Do not contact victim	94
Keep away from victim's home	51
Do not contact victim's family	18
Keep away from victim's workplace	18
Other	19
Total (unweighted n=)	30

Notes:
1.   percentages are proportion of cases with restraining orders in which each type of condition was imposed
2.   unweighted n=30. In five cases information about conditions imposed was not available.

As can be seen from Table 4.4, conditions almost always ordered the offender not to contact the victim in any way.

In all cases in the study in which restraining orders were imposed, the conditions were never altered (although it should be borne in mind that the study's follow-up period was limited and that there might have been subsequent alterations which were not picked up).

It is important that the victim should be informed that an offender has received a restraining order and be aware of the conditions of the order. They can then be alert to any breach of the conditions and take action to inform the police. However, victims in the study maintained that they were rarely informed about the outcome of a trial or whether a restraining order had been imposed. In one case, the lives of an elderly couple had been made very difficult by their not knowing what had happened to a neighbour who had been arrested for harassment and, indeed, whether they could expect the behaviour to start up again at any time. In fact, the offender in this case had been convicted and a restraining order had been imposed, but no one had apparently informed the victims of this.

In the event of a prison sentence being imposed, it is for the court concerned to give full details of the restraining order to the prison authorities so that they can prevent the defendant from contacting the victim from prison. It is quite possible for offenders to continue their course of harassment from prison, usually by telephoning or writing to the victim. Indeed, a restraining order can be made by a court in addition to a prison sentence and is often useful in preventing continuing harassment, as well as ensuring protection of the victim when the offender is released. It should be noted, however, that only a very small minority of defendants convicted for a harassment offence receive a prison sentence, and just two featured in this study.

Breaches of restraining orders

Breach of any of the terms of a restraining order is a triable either way offence which is punishable in the magistrates' court with up to six months imprisonment or a £5,000 fine or both, and in the Crown Court by up to five years imprisonment or an unlimited fine or both. These powers are therefore extremely robust.

In the present study, only one order was known to have been breached, and the defendant was re-arrested and appeared in court. He was bound over for six months in the sum of £250. It is worth noting that data collection was carried out during the latter part of 1999. In the majority of cases, this was about a year after defendants were convicted, whilst 12 defendants had in fact been convicted in 1999. Therefore, there was a limited follow-up period and breaches might have occurred after the period of data collection.

However, although the study provided limited opportunity to follow up cases to monitor breaches of restraining orders and therefore was unlikely to detect many breaches, it appears from interviews with magistrates that very few cases result in offenders appearing before the court for breach. Magistrates accepted that, while their powers to deal with breaches which were brought to their attention were significant, these powers were of little use if there was no effective policing of breaches.

> "Failure of enforcement completely undermines the significance of the order to start with."

> Magistrate

Of course, the absence of breaches brought to the courts' attention might imply that restraining orders are in fact very effective in preventing a repetition of harassment. However, interviews with victims confirmed that breaches of restraining orders certainly do occur.

The issue has already been raised about difficulties that occur where different officers deal with incidents without necessarily being aware of the particulars of the case. Ideally, once a restraining order has been imposed, police called to a subsequent incident should have full knowledge of the conditions of that order. This is not always the case, as is illustrated by an example taken from the study. In this incident, it was left to the victim to provide the police with the information:

"I had to find the restraining order because they didn't know the details and that took about 20 minutes to find…meanwhile, they're waiting outside with him…I would have thought that the police would have to hand a computerised record so that when they come to an address they know about the restraining order."

Victim

Restraining orders were seen by some police respondents as "the cheap way of keeping a suspect away." For this reason, it is important that the police, who have most contact with the victim, collect relevant information during the early stages of the investigation. Some prosecutors referred to the fact that it is the job of the police to discuss details of a potential restraining order with a complainant, in the event of a conviction. The best value from restraining orders can only be derived where as much information as possible about the victim is at hand. Some prosecutors and magistrates maintained that this was often not the case. Indeed, the police were sometimes criticised for not discussing conditions properly with victims. This has obvious implications for the victim if a restraining order is imposed – essentially, the offender might be able to continue with the harassment in a manner which had not been accounted for in the conditions. Every eventuality should be covered in ensuring that the conditions of a potential restraining order are appropriate and that it will therefore be effective. The courts will later rely on this information when putting together an order.

5   Practitioners' views of the Act

The views of practitioners taking part in the study have been used to illustrate issues throughout the report. This chapter explores the interview data more thoroughly.

Advantages of the Act

The police interviewed rated the Act fairly positively as a means of dealing with harassment:

> "[it is] another road we can go down, another string to our bow, if you like to get people before the courts."
>
> Police officer

> "at one time [offenders] used to laugh at us…and all you could say to them was 'will you just leave them alone'…but when we got this Act in then they got a formal warning, then they knew they were going to be locked up."
>
> Police officer

They felt that the Act enabled intervention in cases of harassment where little could be done before. Incidents of harassment may not individually or collectively have amounted to criminal conduct in the past. The comments of police interviewees confirmed that the Act is being widely used for behaviour other than 'stalking' to encompass a range of behaviour stemming from domestic and neighbour disputes. It was considered by some officers that the use of civil injunctions in the county court has probably reduced now that the Protection from Harassment provisions in the criminal court provide an alternative for keeping parties apart.

Both CPS and magistrate interviewees had a number of positive points to make about the Act. The CPS felt that the Act gave them the chance to prosecute in circumstances where they had not always been able to before, and potentially provided protection for victims of harassment. Like the police, lawyers and magistrates believed that the legislation provided greater scope to deal with behaviour which formerly was not well covered by the criminal law and which might previously have been dealt with – if at all – by way of public order or assault charges.

> "It's a nice little Act that covers situations that you know are perhaps individual."
>
> Prosecutor

"There was a big hole, there was nothing, was there?...the police were powerless, the courts were powerless...everyone was powerless, but now we have got some power, let's use it."

Magistrate

Magistrates said that harassment cases form a relatively small proportion of their caseloads, but maintained that they felt confident to deal with them correctly when they did arise. They acknowledged that classic stalking cases were very few and far between, but they felt that there was nothing wrong with the legislation being used to deal with, for example, cases of domestic violence. They argued that protection of the victim was of paramount importance and this was what the Act was designed to achieve.

Some magistrates felt that criminalising harassment cases might lead to unfounded accusations from complainants who are mistaken about another's behaviour or are even vindictive. Prosecutors accepted this point and agreed that they had to be on the lookout for what the police sometimes termed 'paranoid woman syndrome', where the putative victim read more into another's behaviour than was perhaps warranted. However, if they thought that accusations were without foundation, they had scope under the Code for Crown Prosecutors to discontinue proceedings. Ultimately, they agreed that the difficulties in pursuing harassment cases were no greater than other kinds of case – such as domestic violence – where the parties are often well known to each other. In summary, they agreed that the Act benefited victims of harassment considerably.

Restraining orders

"What I am after is the protection of the restraining order .... "

Prosecutor

All those interviewed – CPS, police and magistrates – agreed that restraining orders are effectively 'the teeth' of the Protection From Harassment Act.

"The restraining order is quite a powerful tool to try and keep the peace going."

Police officer

"[victims] don't necessarily want the perpetrators to go to prison, they just want the behaviour to stop and that's what a restraining order can do."

Police officer

Magistrates emphasised the importance of the police and the CPS obtaining sufficient information from complainants about their circumstances in order that an effective restraining order could be imposed. An example illustrates this point. One victim who was interviewed found the offender in her case continued to harass her at work. Whilst one of the conditions forbade the offender to visit the workplace of the victim, the nature of her work regularly required her to drive to other places. The victim often found herself being followed by him. However, the offender was able to continue with the harassment without in fact breaching the restraining order made against him. Had her circumstances been more thoroughly examined, the prosecution might have allowed for this eventuality.

For these reasons, magistrates stressed the importance of thorough collection of information about a complainant's personal circumstances during the early stages of the investigation. The police would be best placed to do this as they have most personal contact with complainants.

Some CPS interviewees felt that orders should automatically be made for an indefinite period of time, in order to provide true protection. Others believed that they should be imposed for long enough to break the cycle of behaviour and that defendants should know the extent of their liability. In this way, a restraining order could provide the victim with the protection that is needed and the offender with "a cooling off period with teeth". Indeed, it was maintained that:

"An unlimited restraining order would just leave skeletons hanging around the cupboard."

Prosecutor

There was a strong belief among CPS respondents that, after some initial uncertainty, magistrates are now well briefed on harassment cases and seem willing to impose restraining orders in the event of a conviction. Indeed, magistrates confirmed that they were more than willing to impose orders if cases came to court, but noted that relatively few actually got that far.

Breaches

The penalties for breaching a restraining order are severe, with up to six months imprisonment in the magistrates' court and up to five years in the Crown Court. Interviews with victims revealed that restraining orders are often breached but allegedly little action is taken by the police in response to this. Some magistrates drew attention to the lack of a clear mechanism for monitoring breaches of restraining orders and bringing them to the court's attention:

"this is good in theory…but has not got enough clout".

Magistrate

One magistrate suggested that 'doorstep curfews' might be effective in addition to a restraining order. These would enable a police officer to turn up at an offender's address at any time without notification to check that they were abiding by their curfew. It was suggested that this might further deter them from breaching conditions.

Some suggested that the remedy of a restraining order might be extended at some point in the future to other kinds of offence, such as assault. For, as has been remarked – notably by Lawson-Cruttenden and Addison (1997) – the anomalous situation exists that a defendant who causes a fear of violence to a victim can be ordered not to contact the victim in that case, whilst someone who actually carries out a violent act cannot be restrained in this way.

However, it is always possible, provided the essential elements of a harassment offence are made out, to add a harassment charge to other charges, thereby providing access to a restraining order.

Shortcomings of the Protection from Harassment Act – criminal or civil proceedings?

This report is primarily concerned with the criminal remedy offered by the Protection from Harassment Act. However, a theme which often arose in interviews was whether the civil remedy contained in the Act might have been more appropriate in some instances. The two remedies were not necessarily intended to cover mutually exclusive types of behaviour. On the whole, police and CPS views differed as to when it was appropriate to use the criminal law rather than the civil remedy, with the police generally tending to favour the former option and the CPS the latter.

"Just one person's word against another, that is not beyond reasonable doubt, that is just a balance of probabilities and would be better suited [to civil law]."

Prosecutor

The broad wording of the legislation was said in some cases to cause confusion, and the police sometimes used the Act where they in fact had doubts about whether it was appropriate to do so. To illustrate this, some practitioners felt that use of the Act to deal with neighbour or domestic disputes was inappropriate and that what were often relatively minor cases might best be dealt with in the Civil Court, albeit at the potential expense of the complainant.[10] While one party might nominally be the complainant, there was often a counter-allegation from the 'offender' and it was sometimes arbitrary which label to apply to which party. Trying to reconcile such cases through the criminal justice system was felt by some to be an impossibility. However, many accepted that there were arguments on both sides. Thus, whilst magistrates could see the benefit of the speedy process in the civil court as compared with the longer trial process in the criminal court, they also tended towards the view that criminalising harassment, however apparently minor, is a more visible or robust way of dealing with such cases and has a more positive impact on the victim.

It certainly appears that the crossover between criminal and civil law in the field of harassment sometimes poses problems. Some prosecutors called for improved police training about when it was appropriate to use the civil rather than the criminal law:

" the line between what is bad [enough] to amount to criminal and what really is civil is a fine line."

Prosecutor

"We are...catching a lot more and wasting a lot of time reviewing files that really shouldn't have been started under the Act."

Prosecutor

"Someone driving past in a car and giving the v-sign – is that really harassment?"

CID officer

A number of other practitioners expressed the view that the Act was intended to deal with the problem of stalkers and is therefore being misused when it is applied to what are seen as relatively minor offences, more fitting for the civil courts.

"It's the genuine stalking cases we've got to proceed with because they result, as we know, in very serious [offences]."

Prosecutor

"You don't criminalise a domestic dispute, unless you know there is a serious problem."

Prosecutor

---

10 If a complainant does not qualify for legal aid, they would have to pay to bring civil proceedings.

The landmark case, which was an important catalyst for the introduction of the Protection from Harassment Act, was that of Tracey Morgan (see Appendix 2). She was stalked for years by an acquaintance and was caused considerable distress thereby. Police officers were often aware of this case and some interpreted harassment as amounting very much to this kind of behaviour. Some felt that these kinds of case were what the Act was originally intended for and felt more inclined to proceed with them than neighbour or domestic disputes.

Charge and prosecution

The CPS in interviews maintained that it was useful to charge section 2 and section 4 as alternatives. One reason was that it was possible to fall back on the section 2 charge in the event that there were difficulties in proving that fear of violence had been caused by the course of behaviour. Since the main aim when prosecuting harassment cases was to prevent a recurrence of the offending behaviour, usually by obtaining a restraining order, prosecutors considered that it often made sense to prosecute for the lesser of the two offences unless there was very clear evidence for a section 4 offence.

Some CPS respondents also mentioned that the police seemed occasionally too ready to use the Act to trigger arrest whether or not they intended to charge a suspect. They also criticised the police for inappropriate charging in harassment cases, and particularly for charging a section 4 offence rather than a section 2 one. For their part, however, the police tended to perceive the CPS as being too ready to downgrade charges. On the face of it, figures in the present study indicated that section 4 charges were more often reduced than section 2 charges were increased (see above). However, the CPS denied this accusation, maintaining that they frequently upgraded charges.

In the light of these contentions, it is revealing to note the view of one magistrate who argued that the problems with coming to terms with this new legislation rest more with the police and the CPS in deciding on appropriate charges and pursuing prosecutions, than with the courts.

"They tend to sort of prosecute under the terms of the law that they have known and loved for years and years."

Magistrate

Ultimately, the police felt that senior officers should tackle the issue of the way in which the Act is being used. In the meantime, they accepted that they could be held accountable if they did not intervene and it was easiest to take the line of least resistance and use the Protection from Harassment Act.

CPS advice

As noted earlier in this report, the police are able if they wish to submit a case file to the CPS for advice on how to proceed, prior to the decision to charge. Advice is typically sought on whether to charge or on the nature and number of charges (Crisp and Moxon, 1994).

CPS respondents felt that they were not approached often enough for pre-charge advice, especially where less straightforward cases were concerned. As a result they believed that they were often put in a bad light when the police laid charges and made promises to a victim about the action that would follow, only to find that the CPS discontinued the case because it was not within the scope of the Act. For these reasons, the Act might be perceived by the CPS as being used inappropriately. Prosecutors argued that this problem might be overcome through the submission of more advice files.

The reluctance of the police to submit files was seen by CPS interviewees as symptomatic of a wider problem of communication. Liaison between the police and CPS was seen as essential to ensure that each was clear about the kind of behaviour which could legitimately fall within the ambit of the Act. To some extent, these perceived problems may have been reduced following the national implementation of the 'Narey' initiative in the magistrates' courts. As part of the measures introduced, the police and CPS liaise at an early stage in the preparation of prosecution files.

Training

Both CPS and police respondents suggested that joint training would be beneficial in order to clear up the kinds of misunderstanding noted above. The CPS appeared to have received more initial training than the police and magistrates in use of the Act. They drew attention to in-house training they had received when the Act first came into force and to handouts which used case studies to give some idea of the kinds of situation in which the Act might be useful.

Magistrates, on the other hand appeared to have received little training, with expertise being developed "on the hoof" as cases came through. Both prosecutors and magistrates felt some degree of frustration with a perceived lack of clear guidance. Of course, training in the event of new legislation is of paramount importance, a view expressed by one magistrate:

"It's the bedrock upon which you can confidently deal with legislation like this."

Magistrate

Magistrates also suggested the need for *police* training in how to deal appropriately with victims of harassment. They thought, for example, that in those harassment cases which were linked with domestic violence it would be advisable for female officers to deal with female complainants. They also advocated further guidance for the police to ensure better policing of breaches of restraining orders.

Most of the police spoken to agreed that more training would be beneficial, although there are obvious constraints on time, as with all practitioners. One suggestion was that specialist persons within forces should become well informed about the Act and impart their knowledge as and when required.

The police believed that they were the ones who were prepared to 'have a go' with harassment cases and that their efforts were often blocked further down the line when cases reached the CPS or the courts. In relation to serious cases reaching the Crown Court, they questioned how aware judges were of the legislation, since their reaction often appeared to be that Protection from Harassment Act cases coming before them should be dealt with in the civil courts.

"...Judges feel that harassment is a civil thing rather than criminal and that becomes quite problematic when we feel, or we are wanting, the backing of the judiciary at a very high level in getting restraining orders and such like and they aren't prepared to assist us and it somewhat knocks us back a bit."

Police training officer

Both the CPS and magistrates felt that there was a lack of knowledge regarding harassment cases among the judiciary. This might not be surprising since very few cases are committed to the Crown Court (only three were found in the present study). Indeed, it was felt that, where the legislation was used, the higher courts tried to confine it to what might be described as the 'classic' stalking situation. Some practitioners suggested that the Lord Chancellor's Department might look at the need for appropriate training for the judiciary in respect of the Protection from Harassment Act.

There were apparent differences between areas regarding training provision for all practitioners. Whether training was provided could depend upon whether there were broader training programmes in place into which guidance on the use of the Act might be incorporated. The difficulties of providing training should be kept in mind, however. With the range of new legislation which is continually being introduced, time and resources may be constraining factors on the depth with which new provisions can be covered.

Mental disorder

CPS interviewees noted that the mental health of a defendant is sometimes raised as an issue in harassment cases. While not a statutory defence, mental health is one factor for the CPS to consider in deciding whether the public interest is served by pursuing a prosecution.

Prosecutors maintained that, unless there is very strong evidence of a mental disorder, they would press ahead with a case:

"Unless a psychiatric report specifically addresses the alleged behaviour in a manner satisfactory to the prosecution, the prosecution will continue."

Note on a harassment file

"Like any crime…we are dealing with the symptom not the source, aren't we, and it is not our usual focus is it, the source?"

Prosecutor

Magistrates believed that the issue of a defendant's mental state was for the court to investigate, rather than the CPS or the police. Magistrates have powers under both the Magistrates Courts Act and the Mental Health Act 1983 to remand defendants either in custody or to hospital for psychiatric reports. If such remands are made before conviction, the magistrates must be satisfied that the accused had committed the act for which he or she has been charged. However, psychiatric assessments of a defendant's mental state can also be arranged as a condition of bail, perhaps via one of the court-based psychiatric assessment schemes that operate around the country. Unless an assessment finds that a defendant is extremely mentally disturbed, these psychiatric assessments are more likely to impact upon sentence rather than conviction. Both prosecutors and magistrates were reluctant to go down the road of diversion from a criminal conviction since this would take away the possibility of a restraining order and, therefore, protection for the victim.

The interests of the victim

Police interviewees maintained that they are generally in regular contact with complainants about their case and are able to keep them informed as to progress. This could be more difficult to do after charge when matters were essentially out of police hands. Victims interviewed certainly felt that they were rarely kept up to date on what was happening with their case and would like to have been better informed.

Practitioners noted the possibility that making a complainant give evidence in court could in itself form part of the harassment perpetrated by the alleged offender.

> "It was like – Oh my God, a) I've got to go into court and be cross-examined and you see it on TV and it's horrible, and b) he's sat there enjoying it knowing he's putting me through it which is all part of the torture."
>
> Tracey Morgan

It has, indeed, been known for defendants to represent themselves and to cross-examine the victim in court. Perhaps due to the fact that harassment cases which come to trial are still relatively uncommon, trials are often covered in the local press. At present, a victim can be named and magistrates argued that there should be an embargo on this in order to lessen distress.

Magistrates were particularly concerned about ways in which the understandable reluctance of victims to give evidence in court might be addressed. One issue they raised was that of better protection of victims in court.[11] One problem with harassment cases is that complainants often do not wish to attend. It had been known in a few cases for a defendant in a Protection from Harassment Act case to become violent in court. Magistrates drew attention to the lack of police presence in court, which might provide a psychological prop for the complainant. However, they had no power to order such attendance.

> "There's nothing like a police officer, as a deterrent or a protection...I have no presence, I have no power."
>
> Magistrate

Most victims felt that they would be happier giving evidence without the defendant being there. Magistrates expressed little enthusiasm for a change in the law so that defendants could be excluded from the courtroom when the victim gave evidence.

---

11 Various provisions have been introduced by the Youth Justice and Criminal Evidence Bill Act 1999, which puts restrictions on the freedom of defendants to personally cross-examine their alleged victims as well as providing measures, such as screens or interviews by video link, to reduce the stress of giving evidence at a trial.

6   Conclusions

This concluding chapter addresses two key issues which have been explored in this report, namely, the way in which the Protection from Harassment Act is being used and its effectiveness in tackling the behaviour at which it is directed.

The use of the Act

There is a widespread perception that the Protection from Harassment Act was introduced to deal with the problem of stalking. However, this study has shown that it is in fact rarely being used for what might be described as 'classic' stalking cases in which a stranger obsessively follows and harasses a person with whom they have become fixated. It is far more often used to deal with a range of lower-level harassment by neighbours and former partners. This raises the question of whether the use of the Act in this way is in fact appropriate. It is relevant to pose this question because a number of practitioners interviewed felt that the effectiveness of the Act was reduced when it was used for what they perceived as relatively low level misconduct at the margins of the criminal law. Their argument was that this would bring the Act into disrepute and that it would cease to be regarded as a viable tool to be used in more serious situations.

In examining these contentions, the first point to consider is what kind of behaviour the Act does actually cover. The legislation is broadly worded and the kind of use being made of it in 'domestic' and neighbour disputes is not necessarily outside the scope of the Act. Types of behaviour other than 'stalking' are clearly encompassed by the Act, in that it specifies that if an offender pursues a course of conduct which causes harassment to another and knows or ought to know that this is harassment (section 2) or puts someone in fear of violence (section 4) he has committed an offence.

However, the argument is not so much that the Act is being applied in situations which do not fall within its ambit than that it is undesirable that it should be used in some of those situations. But it may be the lack of a viable alternative to deal with those situations which is pointing the police (and victims) towards the remedy presented by the Protection from Harassment Act. If there were more satisfactory alternatives, doubtless these would be used. In effect, if there were no legislative hole to fill, then the Act would not be in such widespread use. In this context, the report has pointed to the lack of adequate remedies to deal with harassment prior to the introduction of the Act. An assault charge, for example, would almost always require evidence of physical injury. The available public order provisions lacked teeth or presented difficulties of proof in relation to the offender's intentions. The danger was that serious harm might have resulted to the victim before action could be taken to prevent it. In contrast, the Protection from Harassment Act holds out the prospect of intervention before such harm results. In this sense, therefore, the wider use being made of the Act might appear desirable because it is meeting the need for some sort of intervention to deal with behaviour that annoys and alarms but which has the potential to become more serious.

The points made so far primarily concern the use made of the criminal provisions of the Act. However, the Act also provides for a civil remedy. Those who argued that the criminal provisions are being used inappropriately tended to support the use of the civil remedy to deal with less serious cases involving 'domestic' or neighbour disputes. They suggested that the forms of low level harassment that were sometimes involved were at the margins of the kinds of behaviour with which the criminal law should be concerned. It should be noted, however, that it was never the intention that the criminal and civil remedies should cover mutually exclusive forms of behaviour and in many cases it may be perfectly valid to use either criminal or civil remedy. Because the definition of section 1 applies to both offences of criminal harassment and the civil court, cases involving the Act in the civil courts are as relevant as cases which are dealt with in the criminal courts in defining the offence of criminal harassment.

The fact that the criminal remedy is selected may be for pragmatic reasons. To the police it may be easier to take action to resolve a situation through arrest and charge than by advising the parties about the civil options. Otherwise, they may find that they are subsequently called back on further occasions to deal with a repeat of the same situation. To the victim the civil remedy can present a costly solution if they do not qualify for legal aid, and possibly a complex one. It may, therefore, be cheaper and easier to put the matter in the hands of the police.

However, there may be circumstances in which use of the civil remedy rather than the criminal provisions is appropriate, less because of the kind of behaviour involved than for other reasons. The most obvious is where there are difficulties in proving harassment to the criminal standard of beyond reasonable doubt. The civil burden of the balance of probabilities is easier to satisfy. Another might arise where the victim does not wish to stigmatise the perpetrator with a criminal conviction (perhaps where they are an ex-partner) but wishes to take some action to curtail their harassing behaviour.

It is clear from the above discussion that, whatever the rights and wrongs of the way in which the Act is being used, there is considerable uncertainty in this respect among all practitioners. The net effect has been to foster a degree of inconsistency in decision-making between police, CPS, magistrates and judges (although the last mentioned are involved in relatively few cases). Differences in outlook on the provisions are sometimes found within each of these groups as well as between them. This suggests that there is a need for some form of guidance or clarification from the centre[12] about:

- the kinds of cases which the criminal provisions of the Act are intended to cover

- the circumstances in which the civil remedy might be more appropriate.

These issues might usefully be revisited in any training which police, magistrates, CPS or judges receive in relation to the Protection from Harassment Act.

The effectiveness of the Act

The report has provided a number of pointers to how effectively the Act is being used to deal with harassment. It is as well first of all to be clear about what is meant by 'effectiveness'. It is taken here to mean that:

- the police pursue appropriate action at the right time

- victims are aware of the remedies available to them

- there is a rigorous approach to the prosecution of offenders

- appropriate sentences are passed and executed

- the harassment stops.

Each of these aspects is considered in turn.

---

12 A Home Office document is due to be published in 2000 which provides guidance for investigators on how to deal with harassment cases. It is intended that it should be useful to police dealing with stalking cases as well as other forms of harassment and. It is intended that this guidance be distributed force-wide.

Police action

The police must be clear about what conduct can be taken to constitute harassment within the meaning of the Act and take action at the right time. The research found that these requirements were not always fulfilled. For example, once an instance of possible harassment is brought to their attention, they must wait for a course of conduct to be established in order to make out an offence under the Act. However, some confusion over the issue was apparent. Officers were sometimes found to arrest a suspect after just one incident without first obtaining the necessary proof that there had been a course of conduct.

There are various ways of obtaining such proof. Thus, the police might advise the victim to keep a record of incidents, warn the offender about his or her conduct or make appropriate records of incidents. However, sometimes there was no systematic recording of incidents, or not in a form that was accessible to other officers who might be called to deal with related incidents in the future.

Where a course of conduct was established, the police did not always select the most appropriate charge, sometimes leading to an alteration of charges later on. There was some confusion as to the difference between the section 2 and section 4 offence.

Problems in these respects suggest that there may be a need to review police practice in dealing with harassment incidents with a view to systemising practice to a greater extent and introducing or enhancing training provision. The value of seeking CPS advice when considering whether it is appropriate to charge under section 2 or section 4 (or, indeed, under other legislation) needs to be emphasised in any such review.

Victim awareness

The research found that many victims interviewed were unaware of the availability of the criminal or civil remedies before they called the police. It is also not clear whether victims were aware of the civil option or whether those who did not wish to proceed were aware that this possibility lay open. The implication is that there may be a need for some sort of action, perhaps in the form of a publicity campaign (as with domestic violence), to draw the attention of victims of harassment to the remedies available. The police might also be well placed to give complainants advice about the civil remedy where they decide not to press charges.

Effective prosecution

The study has pointed to the relatively high attrition rate of harassment cases. The cases against 39 per cent of those arrested were dropped. Eight per cent resulted in a bindover after trial rather than a conviction. On the face of it, the high attrition rate does not suggest that cases are being effectively pursued.

One key problem is the extent to which complainants did not wish to proceed with their allegations. This occurred in one-third of cases which were dropped. Faced with the non co-operation of the victim, there is little option but for the CPS to drop the case.

The issue of complainants not wanting to proceed with allegations is not confined to harassment cases but is a common one in cases where there is an existing or former relationship between the alleged offender and the victim. Assaults in domestic violence cases and rape involving intimates or acquaintances are two prime examples. Sometimes, withdrawals occur because the parties become reconciled. But more often it is the prospect of going through the ordeal of a trial which puts complainants off pursuing the case. Attention therefore needs to be given to ways in which victims of harassment may be better supported through the process leading up to trial and the trial itself. The research showed, for example, that victims did not always know what was happening in their case after the suspect had been charged. Better communication may be one step towards encouraging more victims to proceed with their allegations by making them feel more involved. At present, the CPS, who may be best placed to keep victims informed about the progress of a case after charge, do not play a significant role in doing so. However, there are moves afoot to change this situation. The CPS are piloting arrangements recommended in the Glidewell report for direct communication with victims over significant decisions in their case in relation to discontinuance and charge amendment. It is expected that these arrangements will be rolled out nationally next year. In the longer term, it may well be that the CPS will become the lead agency in the provision of information generally to victims and witnesses about the progress of cases after charge.

Attention should also be paid to the role which Victim Support and the Witness Service can play. Victim Support already plays a valuable role in providing moral and other support for victims of a range of offences, although the referral of harassment victims to Victim Support is not mandatory. Although resources are scarce, there are good grounds for arguing, given the number of complainants not wishing to proceed, that harassment victims deserve a high level of attention. For those victims who are required to give evidence, the Witness Service may provide a valuable source of support shortly before and during their court attendance.

Currently, the Witness Service only has a patchy presence in magistrates' courts but is due to expand to cover all courts by 2003. Their efforts should also ensure that fewer victims decide not to proceed with their allegations due to misgivings about giving evidence at trial.

One issue to consider in the context of effective prosecution relates to the preceding section on the use of the Act. A factor in termination of cases and complainants not wishing to proceed may be that the criminal remedy is not always the most appropriate one in the circumstances. If the behaviour in question is at the margins of what the criminal remedy should cover, or if the evidence is not up to the criminal standard, the civil remedy may be more suitable. The termination of such cases may not therefore be inappropriate and could be said to be part of an effective prosecution process. However, this is an argument for ensuring that such cases are not charged in the first place, since termination will almost always lead to dissatisfaction for the victim. The suggestions in the previous section for appropriate use of the criminal sections of the Act by the police would help to ensure that only cases suitable for prosecution are filtered through to the CPS in the first place.

Effective sentencing and prevention of further harassment

While not strictly a sentence, a substantial minority of cases resulted in termination in return for the defendant agreeing to a bindover. Magistrates, in particular, did not consider that this was an effective means of prevention and felt that it was a relatively toothless disposal. There was general agreement among practitioners that the most important aspect of the Act is the restraining order (not available with a bindover). Victims are primarily concerned that the harassment ceases and for the court to be able to order an offender to stay away from them should ensure the protection that they seek. Some practitioners in the present study were so enthusiastic about restraining orders that they argued for the ability to impose them for certain other offences.

Given the perceived value of restraining orders, however, it is perhaps surprising that they were only imposed in around half of convictions. It is not clear why they were not used in almost all cases. It might reflect a belief in traditional measures and/or lack of faith in the new. Some practitioners appeared ignorant of the new measures. Others may have felt that they were too draconian in some cases of a less serious nature. Sometimes prosecutors may have failed to raise the issue of a restraining order.

On the face of it, there appear to be some grounds for considering whether restraining orders could not, with benefit, be deployed as a matter of course. However, this begs the question of whether they do in fact achieve what they are intended to: a cessation of harassment. The research was unable to provide firm statistical data on this point because there was limited time between the date that restraining orders were imposed and the time that data were collected to allow adequate follow-up. However, the available data, primarily from interviews, suggests that restraining orders are breached relatively often and that there are problems with their enforcement.

Based on the evidence provided by the research, a number of suggestions might be put forward for enhancing the effectiveness of restraining orders.

- Firstly, it is important that the police collect as much relevant information as possible about the circumstances of the case so that, when it comes to framing a restraining order, it can be worded in a way that fully confronts the range of behaviour that was the source of distress to the victim. To ensure maximum effectiveness, discussions with the victim about the order are likely to be invaluable.

- Secondly, once an order is made, the victim needs to be told what the conditions of the order are so that they will know whether a breach has occurred.

- Thirdly, victims should be clear about what they should do when there is a breach in terms of reporting to the police.

- Fourthly, the police need to ensure that there is centralised recording of restraining orders and that officers covering an area are aware of those orders and any new ones issued.

- Lastly, the police should be left in no doubt of the importance of actively seeking to identify breaches of orders. The heavy penalties that may potentially follow a breach make it amply clear how seriously such breaches should be regarded and policing of breaches should be treated with commensurate seriousness.

The suggestions made in this chapter clearly carry training implications. For all agencies there are issues relating to awareness of restraining orders which need to be addressed, so that maximum effective use is made of them. And for the police there are practical issues relating to the collection of information relevant to the framing of orders and the effective enforcement of orders once issued.

Appendix 1

Section 1 – Prohibition of harassment

(1) A person must not pursue a course of conduct –

(a) which amounts to harassment of another, and
(b) which he knows or ought to know amounts to harassment of the other.

Section 2 – Criminal harassment (summary offence[13])

(1) A person who pursues a course of conduct in breach of section 1 is guilty of an offence.

Section 4 – Fear of violence (either-way offence[14])

(1) A person whose course of conduct causes another to fear, on at least two occasions, that violence will be used against him is guilty of an offence if he knows or ought to know that his course of conduct will cause the other so to fear on each of those occasions.

(2) For the purposes of this section, the person whose course of conduct is in question ought to know that it will cause another to fear that violence will be used against him on any occasion if a reasonable person in possession of the same information would think the course of conduct would cause the other so to fear on that occasion.

---

13 punishable by six months in prison or a maximum fine of #£5,000 or both.
14 punishable by up to five years in prison or an unlimited fine or both.

Protection from Harassment Act 1997

1997 Chapter 40 – *continued*

An Act to make provision for protecting persons from harassment and similar conduct.

[21st March 1997]

BE IT ENACTED by the Queen's most Excellent Majesty, by and with the advice and consent of the Lords Spiritual and Temporal, and Commons, in this present Parliament assembled, and by the authority of the same, as follows:-

England and Wales

Prohibition of harassment   1. – (1) A person must not pursue a course of conduct-

(a) which amounts to harassment of another, and

(b) which he knows or ought to know amounts to harassment of the other.

(2) For the purposes of this section, the person whose course of conduct is in question ought to know that it amounts to harassment of another if a reasonable person in possession of the same information would think the course of conduct amounted to harassment of the other.

(3) Subsection (1) does not apply to a course of conduct if the person who pursued it shows-

(a) that it was pursued for the purpose of preventing or detecting crime,

(b) that it was pursued under any enactment or rule of law or to comply with any condition or requirement imposed by any person under any enactment, or

(c) that in the particular circumstances the pursuit of the course of conduct was reasonable.

Offence of harassment.

2. – (1) A person who pursues a course of conduct in breach of section 1 is guilty of an offence.

(2) A person guilty of an offence under this section is liable on summary conviction to imprisonment for a term not exceeding six months, or a fine not exceeding level 5 on the standard scale, or both.

(3) In section 24(2) of the Police and Criminal Evidence Act 1984 (arrestable offences), after paragraph (m) there is inserted-

"(n) an offence under section 2 of the Protection from Harassment Act 1997 (harassment)."

Civil remedy.

3. – (1) An actual or apprehended breach of section 1 may be the subject of a claim in civil proceedings by the person who is or may be the victim of the course of conduct in question.

(2) On such a claim, damages may be awarded for (among other things) any anxiety caused by the harassment and any financial loss resulting from the harassment.

(3) Where –

(a) in such proceedings the High Court or a county court grants an injunction for the purpose of restraining the defendant from pursuing any conduct which amounts to harassment, and

(b) the plaintiff considers that the defendant has done anything which he is prohibited from doing by the injunction,

the plaintiff may apply for the issue of a warrant for the arrest of the defendant.

(4) An application under subsection (3) may be made-

(a) where the injunction was granted by the High Court, to a judge of that court, and

(b) where the injunction was granted by a county court, to a judge or district judge of that or any other county court.

(5) The judge or district judge to whom an application under subsection (3) is made may only issue a warrant if-

(a) the application is substantiated on oath, and

(b) the judge or district judge has reasonable grounds for believing that the defendant has done anything which he is prohibited from doing by the injunction.

(6) Where-

(a) the High Court or a county court grants an injunction for the purpose mentioned in subjection (3)(a), and

(b) without reasonable excuse the defendant does anything which he is prohibited from doing by the injunction, he is guilty of an offence.

(7) Where a person is convicted of an offence under subsection (6) in respect of any conduct which has been punished as a contempt of court.

(8) A person cannot be convicted of an offence under subsection (6) in respect of any conduct which has been punished as a contempt of court.

(9) A person guilty of an offence under subsection (6) is liable-

(a) on conviction on indictment, to imprisonment for a term not exceeding five years, or a fine, or both, or

(b) on summary conviction, to imprisonment for a term not exceeding six months, or a fine not exceeding the statutory maximum, or both.

Putting people in fear of violence.

4. – (1) A person whose course of conduct causes another to fear, on at least two occasions, that violence will be used against him is guilty of an offence if he knows or ought to know that his course of conduct will cause the other so to fear on each of those occasions.

(2) For the purposes of this section, the person whose course of conduct is in question ought to know that it will cause another to fear that violence will be used against him on any occasion if a reasonable person in possession of the same information would think the course of conduct would cause the other so to fear on that occasion.

(4) It is a defence for a person charged with an offence under this section to show that-

(a) his course of conduct was pursued for the purpose of preventing or detecting crime,

(b) his course of conduct was pursued under any enactment or rule of law or to comply with any condition or requirement imposed by any person under any enactment, or

(c) the pursuit of his course of conduct was reasonable for the protection of himself or another or for the protection of his or another's property.

(4) A person guilty of an offence under this section is liable-

(a) on conviction on indictment, to imprisonment for a term not exceeding five years, or a fine, or both, or

(b) on summary conviction, to imprisonment for a term not exceeding six months, or a fine not exceeding the statutory maximum, or both.

(5) If on the trial on indictment of a person charged with an offence under this section the jury find him not guilty of the offence charged, they may find him guilty of an offence under section 2.

(6) The Crown Court has the same powers and duties in relation to a person who is by virtue of subsection (5) convicted before it of an offence under section 2 as a magistrates' court would have on convicting him of the offence.

Restraining orders. 5. – (1) A court sentencing or otherwise dealing with a person ("the defendant") convicted of an offence under section 2 or 4 may (as well as sentencing him or dealing with him in any other way) make an order under this section.

(2) The order may, for the purpose of protecting the vi time of the offence, or any other person mentioned in the order, from further conduct which –

(a) amounts to harassment, or

(b) will cause a fear of violence,

prohibit the defendant from doing anything described in the order.

(3) The order may have effect for a specified period or until further order.

(4) The prosecutor, the defendant or any other person mentioned in the order may apply to the court which made the order for it to be varied or discharged by a further order.

(5) If without reasonable excuse the defendant does anything which he is prohibited from doing by an order under this section, he is guilty of an offence.

(6) A person guilty of an offence under this section is liable –

(a) on conviction on indictment, to imprisonment for a term not exceeding five years, or a fine, or both, or

(b) on summary conviction, to imprisonment for a term not exceeding the statutory maximum, or both.

Limitation.

6. In section 11 of the Limitation Act 1980 (special time limit for actions in respect of personal injuries), after subsection (1) there is inserted-

"(1A) This section does not apply to any action brought for damages under section 3 of the Protection from Harassment Act 1997".

Interpretation of this group of Sections.

7. – (1) This section applies for the interpretation of sections 1 to 5.

(2) References to harassing a person include alarming the person or causing the person distress.

(3) A "course of conduct" must involve conduct on at least two occasions.

(4) "Conduct" includes speech.

Appendix 2

The case of R v Burstow (1996)

The criminal behaviour of Mr Burstow towards Ms Morgan began on 26 October 1992, when both he and Ms Morgan were members of the Navy, with the unauthorised entry of the defendant into Ms Morgan's residence and the theft of her lingerie. One of the predisposing features in the stalking of Ms Morgan was Mr Burstow's divorce from his wife (also called Tracey) in July, 1993. Mr Burstow turned to Ms Morgan as a confidante and a friend, she being happily married. Mr Burstow has claimed that there was a sexual relationship between them, initially.

As part of the harassment, Mr Burstow engaged in behaviour which was usually demeaning towards Ms Morgan. As the harassment continued, Ms Morgan went from being idealised to being devalued in the eyes of her perpetrator.

Even once Ms Morgan had left the Navy, Mr Burstow embarked on a continued campaign of 'passive' harassment, seeking to ensure that he did not commit an overt act which might constitute an offence. The course of conduct included: the victim being followed; silent telephone calls; personal items being interfered with or taken from her home; use of a scanner to track/monitor telephone messages between the victim and police as well as to listen to conversations within her home; interference with Ms Morgan's bank account; allegedly hiring a hit-man to kill her husband (the man went to the police); harassment of family and friends; changing his name to that of an ex-partner of hers.

At the time the harassment started (1992), the behaviour was reported to officers in the Navy. The police became involved in 1993. Two officers, in particular, were involved in the case and appreciated the problems implicated in dealing with such a case under current law. These officers were in fact responsible for taking the case to the government suggesting a change in the law. This campaign ultimately resulted in the Protection from Harassment Act.

During the course of the campaign of harassment against Ms Morgan, Mr Burstow was convicted of a range of offences arising from his behaviour. Many of the offences are still good in law and similar prosecutions can still be mounted under them. These convictions included: two offences of criminal damage and several incidences of burglary, breach of the peace, misuse of a scanner and Misuse of the Telecommunications Act. Some telephone calls were traced to his prison wing at a time when the offender was incarcerated.

The decision in R v Burstow (1996) (The Times, 30 July), established the doctrine of psychological assault, enabling a defendant to be convicted of assault even where there has been no direct physical force. Tracey Morgan has campaigned to extend the law to the automatic referral of those arrested under the Protection from Harassment Act for psychiatric assessment. She claims that this would identify psychological or personality disorders early on in the system. This is the case with suspects of harassment in America.

Appendix 3

National statistics on the Protection from Harassment Act 1997

The Act came into force on 16 June 1997. Statistics on cautions and court proceedings for 1998 and 1999 are presented in this Appendix. The 1999 figures are provisional and cover only the first nine months for magistrates' courts.

Cautions

In 1998, 693 people were cautioned for an offence under s2 of the Act and 173 for an offence under s4. The 1999 figures were 983 and 165 respectively. For the racially aggravated offences which came into force on 30 June 1998, there were 36 cautions in 1999 for the s2 offence and 15 for the s4 offence.

Court proceedings

The number of persons proceeded against in magistrates' courts for s2 and s4 offences in 1998 and the first nine months of 1999 are given in Table A3.1. In addition, there were 23 people proceeded against in 1998 for breach of an injunction against harassment (s3) and 357 for breach of a restraining order (s4). The corresponding figures for the first nine months of 1999 were 24 and 471.

There were 62 persons proceeded against for the racially aggravated s2 offence in the first nine months of 1999 and 45 for the racially aggravated s4 offence.

Sentencing

The distribution of sentencing at magistrates' courts and the Crown Court is given in Table A3.2.

In total 733 of those sentenced at magistrates' courts in 1998 were given a restraining order (mostly in addition to a sentence). The provisional figure for 1999 was 1,057. A further 37 restraining orders were given out in the Crown Court in 1998 and 111 in 1999.

Table A3.1: **Number of persons proceeded against at magistrates' courts for offences under the Protection from Harassment Act 1997 by type of offence and result, England and Wales 1998 and 1999 (p)**

	Total number proceeded against	Terminated early	Committed for trial	At magistrates' court Dismissed	At magistrates' court Found Guilty	Committed for sentence
Summary offence of harassment (S2)						
1998	4,304	1,821	6	312	2,165	10
1999 (Jan–Sept)	3,813	1,700	6	240	1,867	10
Putting people in fear of violence (S4)						
1998	1,505	852	171	62	420	31
1999 (Jan–Sept)	1,176	684	145	66	281	15

Table A3.2: Sentencing at court for offences under the Protection from Harassment Act 1997 by type of offence and result, England and Wales 1998 and 1999 (p)

	Total sentenced (=100%)	Discharge	Fine	Sentence	Community Custody	Other
Magistrates' courts						
Summary offence of harassment (S2)						
1998	2,155	35%	24%	26%	10%	5%
1999	1,857	37%	21%	26%	11%	5%
(Jan – Sept)						
Putting people in fear of violence (S4)						
1998	389	25%	16%	40%	15%	3%
1999	266	20%	23%	40%	14%	4%
(Jan – Sept)						
Crown Court						
Summary offence of harassment (S2)						
1998	69	12%	6%	36%	38%	9%
1999	90	21%	7%	46%	21%	6%
Putting people in fear of violence (S4)						
1998	125	7%	2%	30%	50%	10%
1999	126	8%	4%	34%	46%	8%

(p) = provisional

References

Crisp, D. and Moxon, D. (1994) *Case screening by the Crown Prosecution Service:* How and why cases are terminated. Home Office Research Study No. 137

Crown Prosecution Service (1996) *Code for Crown Prosecutors.* London: CPS

Farnham, F.R., James, D.V. and Cantrell, P. (2000) *Association between violence, psychosis and relationship to victim in stalkers* The Lancet, Vol 355, January 15 2000

Harris, J. and Grace, S. (1999) *A question of evidence? Investigating and prosecuting rape in the 1990s* Home Office Research Study 196

Hoyle, C., Cape, E., Morgan, R. and Sanders, A. (1998) *Evaluation of the 'One Stop Shop' and victim statement pilot projects* A report for the Home Office Research Development and Statistics Directorate

Lawson-Cruttenden, T. and Addison, N. (1997) *Blackstone's Guide to the Protection from Harassment Act 1997* Blackstone Press Ltd

Mullen, P., Pathe M., Purcell, R. and Stuart, G.W. *Study of stalkers* (1999) American Journal of Psychiatry, 156: 1244-49

Meloy, J.R. Stalking: *An old behaviour, a new crime* (1999) Forensic Psychiatry No.1

Meloy, J.R. (1997) *The clinical risk management of stalking: "Someone is watching over me..."* American Journal of Psychotherapy, vol 51, No.2, Spring 1997

Meloy, J.R. and Gothard, S. (1995) *Demographic and clinical comparison of obsessional followers and offenders with mental disorders* American Journal of psychiatry, 152, 258-263

Tjaden, P. *The crime of stalking: How big is the problem?* Summary of a presentation, National institute of Justice

Zona, M., Sharma, K. and Lane, J.A. *A comparative study of erontomanic and obsessional subjects in a forensic sample* (1993) Journal of Forensic Science 38: 894-903

Zona, M.A., Palarea, R.E. and Lance, J.C. *Psychiatric diagnosis and the offender-victim typology of stalking* In Meloy J.R. (ed) The psychology of stalking San Diego : Academic Press (1998)

RDS Publications

Requests for Publications

Copies of our publications and a list of those currently available may be obtained from:

> Home Office
> Research, Development and Statistics Directorate
> Communications Development Unit
> Room 201, Home Office
> 50 Queen Anne's Gate
> London SW1H 9AT
> Telephone: 020 7273 2084 (answerphone outside of office hours)
> Facsimile: 020 7222 0211
> E-mail: publications.rds@homeoffice.gsi.gov.uk

alternatively

why not visit the RDS web-site at
> Internet: http://www.homeoffice.gov.uk/rds/index.htm

where many of our publications are availabe to be read on screen or downloaded for printing.